THE AGE OF REVOLUTION

THE

AMERICAN REVOLUTION

LIFE, LIBERTY, AND THE PURSUIT OF HAPPINESS

EDITED BY
ZOE LOWERY

Britannica
Educational Publishing
IN ASSOCIATION WITH

ROSEN
EDUCATIONAL SERVICES

Published in 2016 by Britannica Educational Publishing (a trademark of Encyclopædia Britannica, Inc.) in association with The Rosen Publishing Group, Inc.
29 East 21st Street, New York, NY 10010

Distributed exclusively by Rosen Publishing.
To see additional Britannica Educational Publishing titles, go to rosenpublishing.com.

First Edition

Britannica Educational Publishing
J. E. Luebering: Director, Core Reference Group
Anthony L. Green: Editor, Compton's by Britannica

Rosen Publishing
Hope Lourie Killcoyne: Executive Editor
Zoe Lowery: Editor
Nelson Sá: Art Director
Brian Garvey: Designer
Cindy Reiman: Photography Manager
Introduction and supplementary material by Norman Graubart

Library of Congress Cataloging-in-Publication Data

The American Revolution: life, liberty, and the pursuit of happiness/edited by Zoe Lowery.—First edition.
    pages cm.—(The age of revolution)
Includes bibliographical references and index.
ISBN 978-1-68048-020-7 (library bound)
1. United States—History—Revolution, 1775–1783—Juvenile literature. I. Lowery, Zoe.
E208.A435 2015
973.3—dc23
                                2014041869

Manufactured in the United States of America

CONTENTS

CONTENTS

CHAPTER 4

THE SOCIAL REVOLUTION AND THE NEW REPUBLIC

CHAPTER 5

CONTENTS

"I have never met with a man, either in England or America, who hath not confessed his opinion, that a separation between the countries, would take place at one time or other..."

—Thomas Paine, from *Common Sense*

We often think of the American Revolution as being predestined, or bound to happen. But was it indeed inevitable? Thomas Paine, an English pamphleteer who lived most of his life in the 13 colonies, seemed to think so. To him, England was a nation of backwardness. He believed that the system of monarchy made it very easy for the population to understand where all of their problems came from (the king), but it also made them unable to fix their problems in a rational manner through government. As the colonists became more self-sufficient, they began to lose their affection with this system, just as Paine had. Those who would follow this line of reasoning and support independence were called patriots.

But not all colonists were patriots. Loyalists believed, even well into the Revolutionary War, that the colonies should remain with England. There were many reasons for this. It's important to remember that, before the Revolution, the colonists were subjects of the British Empire. This meant that they were not citizens of a republic but in fact owed their

Thomas Paine (1737–1809) was a political writer whose papers, such as Common Sense, spurred Americans into action and, ultimately, revolution.

very existence and their human rights to the king and queen of England. Most of these subjects shared their church, their language, and their traditions with England. Those subjects who cared about these connections more than taxes were likely to become loyalists. To be a patriot was to have faith and hope that breaking these historical connections would be a reasonable price to pay for establishing a republic.

But were the forces of loyalism and patriotism bound to fight each other in the end? Could there have been a compromise? This is where the preceding Paine quotation becomes revealing. It was not just the colonists or the patriots who saw the Revolution coming. Paine makes no such distinctions in his statement. According to him, all men both in England and America believe that "a separation [will] take place at one time or other." This statement alone was neither an endorsement nor repudiation of the Revolution (although Paine was perhaps the most ardent patriot writer) but an observation about both the English and American political environments of the time. In other words, whether you wanted revolution or you wanted to keep the relationship with Britain, the news of the day forced you to have an opinion. And the news was revolution.

Whether or not the Revolution itself was inevitable, it's certainly true that the Revolution could have failed. This resource recounts a great deal of military history, beginning with the battles of Lexington and Concord in 1776 and ending with the Treaty of Paris in 1783. It also covers the young, untested general named George Washington and the intimidating British figure of Lord Cornwallis. While it might be something of a cliché to say that the American Revolution was a war waged "against all odds," this is in fact the case. Had France not offered its help, had the British been more strategic militarily, and had the colonists been less sure of their cause, the Revolution could have been easily squashed. While the colonists knew their territory better than the British, they were largely unskilled and lacked the order and sophistication of the British army. Furthermore, this resource will discuss how the British failed to win the war by failing to devise a strategy that could outsmart and outkill the driven revolutionaries.

To be sure, the American Revolution was not a sudden earthquake or volcanic eruption. It had its causes and could perhaps have had several different outcomes. But the conflict over something as mundane as taxes put several social forces up against each other in plain view. Now, the idea of self-government was put squarely in opposition to the concept of autocratic, hereditary monarchy. The idea of a state church withered in a vast network of diverse colonial states and communities, where religious revivals and new branches of Christianity were thriving against the official backdrop of a distant, hierarchical Anglican Church.

It's difficult to overstate the degree to which arguments about religion helped forge the young republic. Deism is a religious belief that grew popular during the Enlightenment. Paine, Thomas Jefferson, Benjamin Franklin, and George Washington were all deists of one stripe or another. The central idea of Deism is that there must have been a god that set the universe in motion and created everything in it, but that this being does not intervene in current affairs. This was a radical view during a time when most Western governments were closely allied to their respective churches, most of which were hostile to Deism.

Secularism, or the separation of church and state, would come to have many interesting effects on the young country. It didn't lead to mass atheism or hostility toward faith. Just as the deists were authoring the founding documents of the republic, Baptists, Congregationalists, Methodists, Presbyterians, Jews, Catholics, and other faith groups were building their own houses of worship in every town, taking their religion to the frontier, and forming new denominations. While the previous three centuries in Europe had seen a nearly continuous stream of bloodshed over religious conflict, religious pluralism enshrined in law was allowing America to thrive.

But the Revolution wasn't just the product of broad social forces. Several men and women are still honored both in America and around the world for the crucial roles they played in the Revolution. This resource delves into their own personal histories as well as their professional lives. You may have heard of John Adams, the nation's second president. But, what about his wife, Abigail? This resource includes a detailed account of her life as the manager of the Adams family farm and other financial interests that were crucial to John's success. She also wrote passionately to her husband about a woman's right to education nearly a century before the first American state allowed women the right to vote. If her protestations did not amount to much success in the late 1700s, there can be no doubt that Abigail Adams's life and words foreshadowed some of the great social movements of the 19th and 20th centuries.

Not all the early Americans who shaped the early country became as famous or legendary as the Founders. This resource profiles certain figures such as Mary Otis Warren, who wrote plays and poems that dramatized current events so that ordinary colonists could identify with the struggle. It also discusses Thomas Paine, the man quoted at the beginning of this introduction, whose criticism of religion has marginalized his influence in some textbooks. Read on to learn about local politicians, military heroes, and other ordinary people who took a chance on Revolution and changed the course of history.

The American Revolution created as many problems as it tried to solve. One of these questions bitterly divided the members of the First and Second Continental Congresses—the relationship between the provisional states and the provisional federal government. Federalists, like Alexander Hamilton and James Madison, believed that the new government should be centralized, with the legal and economic boundaries between the states more or less erased. Anti-Federalists, such as Thomas Jefferson and George Mason, wanted the states to be more independent from federal power. Ultimately, a national bank was created, showing that the Federalists held sway over monetary policy. But, when the Civil War erupted 80 years later, Americans would be brutally reminded of just how different the states were from one another. States that were close to each other geographically, that spoke the same language, and used the same money, were willing to fight each other during the Civil War over the question of slavery. Although the slavery question was ultimately settled, reading or watching the news today should quickly remind you how some fundamental questions are still debated today. Debates over health care, taxes, and immigration continue to put the questions of state and federal power in the front of our minds. The United States has become a powerful and successful country, however, citizens still fiercely argue with one other about what kind of country it is, or should be. This is due in large part to the arguments laid out and exchanged by the founders. It serves as evidence that the act of revolution is not sufficient to building a society. The arguments, tensions, and struggles that fuel a revolution must also continue in the new state.

The system described previously is called liberal democracy. It is the kind of system in which heated disagreements, ideological battles, and political struggles can play themselves out without rupturing the most basic structures of society. It is hard to imagine, in retrospect, what the world might look like without this phenomenon. After all, there are now many countries in the world that follow our example to some degree or another. France, which had been a monarchy for nearly a millennium, had a revolution just a few years after the American one. In fact, Thomas Paine, Thomas Jefferson, and John Adams (among others), engaged in serious debates about that Revolution and what its causes and effects might be. Both the French Revolution itself and the debates that it sparked in both Britain and the new United States helped usher in the new era of liberal democracy. What this term means and how it can be applied to different societies around the world is still one of the great questions.

The greatest failure of the American Revolution was the postponing of the slavery question. This resource makes clear why this happened. Aside from the fact that Washington, Jefferson, and Madison were slaveholders, many of the founders believed that there was no practical way of abolishing slavery without putting the newborn nation in jeopardy. Nevertheless, the brighter of the Enlightenment men and women contained within them the seeds of abolition. They were conscious of this, too. Washington, who had amassed a fortune on the backs of his slaves, freed them upon his death. More importantly, the words the founders put in the Constitution would be quoted no less than half a century later, when the abolitionist movement began to capture America's soul. Frederick Douglass and other brave abolitionists would not claim that America was doomed because of slavery, but instead argued that the nation could in fact be saved because of the ringing words of the Constitution and the promise of liberty.

So, in returning to Thomas Paine's assertion, was this Revolution inevitable? Did all of these social forces have to play out on the battlefield? Could not this diverse group of reasonable men have forged some kind of mutually beneficial deal with Britain instead of starting a costly war whose outcome was unclear? One certainly wonders what that compromise might have looked like. The example of slavery provides an insight. The compromises made over slavery and the postponement of abolition would tear the nation apart by the 1860s. In political circles, this is called "kicking the can down the road." There are certainly some questions that must eventually be answered—some scores that must be settled. In his immortal Gettysburg Address, Abraham Lincoln would allude to abolition, the reassertion of human liberty, as the "new birth of freedom." Hopefully this resource will help readers understand the causes, effects, and nature of America's original birth of freedom, the America Revolution, and help them draw their own conclusions about these still-discussed questions.

PRELUDE TO A REVOLUTION

Britain's victory over France in the Great War for the Empire had been won at very great cost. British government expenditures, which had amounted to nearly £6.5 million annually before the war, rose to about £14.5 million annually during the war. As a result, the burden of taxation in England was probably the highest in the country's history, much of it borne by the politically influential landed classes. Furthermore, with the acquisition of the vast domain of Canada and the prospect of holding British territories both against the various nations of Indians and against the Spaniards to the south and west, the costs of colonial defense could be expected to continue indefinitely. Parliament, moreover, had voted to give Massachusetts a generous sum in compensation for its war expenses. It therefore seemed reasonable to British opinion that some of the future burden of payment should be shifted to the colonists themselves—who until then had been lightly taxed and indeed lightly governed.

The prolonged wars had also revealed the need to tighten the administration of the loosely run and widely scattered elements of the British Empire. If the course of the war had confirmed the necessity, the end of the war presented the opportunity. The acquisition of Canada required officials in London to take responsibility for the unsettled western territories, now freed from the threat of French occupation. The British soon moved to take charge of the whole field of Indian relations. By the royal Proclamation of 1763, a line was drawn down the Appalachians marking the limit of settlement from the British colonies, beyond which Indian trade was to be conducted strictly through British-appointed commissioners. The proclamation sprang in part from a respect for Indian rights (though it did not come in time to prevent the uprising led by Pontiac). From London's viewpoint, leaving a lightly garrisoned West to the fur-gathering Indians also made economic and imperial sense. The proclamation, however, caused consternation among British colonists for two reasons. It meant that limits were being set to the prospects of settlement and speculation in western lands, and it took control of the west out of colonial hands. The most ambitious men in the colonies thus saw the proclamation as a loss of power to control their own fortunes. Indeed, the British government's huge underestimation of how deeply the halt in westward expansion would be resented by the colonists was one of the factors in sparking the 12-year crisis that led to the American Revolution. Indian efforts to preserve a terrain for themselves in the continental interior might still have had a chance with British policy makers, but they would be totally ineffective when the time came to deal with a triumphant United States of America.

PROCLAMATION OF 1763

The Proclamation of 1763 was a proclamation declared by the British crown at the end of the French and Indian War in North America, mainly intended to conciliate the Indians by checking the encroachment of settlers on their lands. In the centuries since the proclamation, it has become one of the cornerstones of Native American law in the United States and Canada.

After Indian grievances had resulted in the start of Pontiac's War (1763-64), British authorities determined to subdue intercolonial rivalries and abuses by dealing with Indian problems as a whole. To this end, the proclamation organized new British territories in America—the provinces of Quebec, East and West Florida, and Grenada (in the Windward Islands)—and a vast British-administered Indian reservation west of the Appalachians, from south of Hudson Bay to north of the Floridas. It forbade settlement on Indian territory, ordered those settlers already there to withdraw, and strictly limited future settlement. For the first time in the history of European colonization in the New World, the proclamation formalized the concept of Indian land titles, prohibiting issuance of patents to any lands claimed by a tribe unless the Indian title had first been extinguished by purchase or treaty.

Although not intended to alter western boundaries, the proclamation was nevertheless offensive to the colonies as undue interference in their affairs. Treaties following Pontiac's War drew a line of settlement more acceptable to colonial settlers, but the continued westward movement of pioneers, and the settlers' disregard of the proclamation's provisions evoked decades of continued Indian warfare throughout the area. The addition of the balance of territory north of the Ohio River to Quebec in 1774 further exacerbated colonial conflict with Britain.

THE TAX CONTROVERSY

George Grenville, who was named prime minister in 1763, was soon looking to meet the costs of defense by raising revenue in the colonies. The first measure was the Plantation Act of 1764, usually called the Revenue, or Sugar, Act, which reduced to a mere threepence the duty on imported foreign molasses but linked with this a high duty on refined sugar and a prohibition on foreign rum (the needs of the British treasury were carefully balanced with those of West Indies planters and New England distillers). The last measure of this kind (1733) had not been enforced, but this time the government set up a system of customs houses, staffed by British officers, and even established a vice-admiralty court. The court sat at Halifax, N.S., and heard very few cases, but in principle it appeared to threaten the cherished British privilege of trials by local juries. Boston further objected to the tax's revenue-raising aspect on constitutional

ENGLISH POLITICIAN GEORGE GRENVILLE'S POLICY OF TAXING THE AMERICAN COLONIES FUELED THE TRAIN OF EVENTS LEADING TO THE AMERICAN REVOLUTION.

grounds, but, despite some expressions of anxiety, the colonies in general acquiesced.

Parliament next affected colonial economic prospects by passing a Currency Act (1764) to withdraw paper currencies, many of them surviving from the war period, from circulation. This was not done to restrict economic growth so much as to take out currency that was thought to be unsound, but it did severely reduce the circulating medium during the difficult postwar period and further indicated that such matters were subject to British control.

Grenville's next move was a stamp duty, to be raised on a wide variety of transactions, including legal writs, newspaper advertisements, and ships' bills of lading. The colonies were duly consulted and offered no alternative suggestions. The feeling in London, shared by Benjamin Franklin, was that, after making formal objections, the colonies would accept the new taxes as they had the earlier ones. But the Stamp Act (1765) hit harder and deeper than any previous parliamentary measure. As some agents had already pointed out, because of postwar economic difficulties the colonies were short of ready funds. (In Virginia this shortage was so serious that the province's treasurer, John Robinson, who was also speaker of the assembly, manipulated and redistributed paper money that had been officially withdrawn from circulation by the Currency Act; a large proportion of the landed gentry benefited from this largesse.) The Stamp Act struck at vital points of colonial economic operations, affecting transactions in trade. It also affected many of the most articulate and influential people in the colonies (lawyers, journalists, bankers). It was, moreover, the first "internal" tax levied directly on the colonies by Parliament. Previous colonial taxes had been levied by local authorities or had been "external" import duties whose primary aim could be viewed as regulating trade for the benefit of the empire as a whole rather than raising revenue. Yet no one, either in Britain or in the colonies, fully anticipated the uproar that followed the imposition of these duties. Mobs in Boston and other towns rioted and forced appointed stamp distributors to renounce their posts; legal business was largely halted. Several colonies sent delegations to a Congress in New York in the summer of 1765, where the Stamp Act was denounced as a violation of the Englishman's right to be taxed only through elected representatives, and plans were adopted to impose a nonimportation embargo on British goods.

A change of ministry facilitated a change of British policy on taxation. Parliamentary opinion was angered by what it perceived as colonial lawlessness, but British merchants were worried about the embargo on British imports. The marquis of Rockingham, succeeding Grenville, was persuaded to repeal the Stamp Act—for domestic reasons rather than out of any sympathy with colonial protests—and in 1766 the repeal was passed. On the same day, however, Parliament also passed the Declaratory Act, which declared that Parliament had the power to bind or legislate the colonies "in all cases whatsoever." Parliament would not have voted the repeal without this assertion of its authority.

The colonists, jubilant at the repeal of the Stamp Act, drank innumerable toasts, sounded peals of cannon, and were prepared to ignore the Declaratory Act as face-saving window dressing. John Adams, however, warned in his *Dissertation on the Canon and Feudal Law* that Parliament, armed with this view of its powers, would try to tax the colonies again; and this happened in 1767 when Charles Townshend became chancellor of the Exchequer in a ministry formed by Pitt, now earl of Chatham. The problem was that Britain's financial burden had not been lifted. Townshend, claiming to take literally the colonial distinction between external and internal taxes, imposed external duties on a wide range of necessities, including lead, glass, paint, paper, and tea, the principal domestic beverage. One ominous result was that colonists now began to believe that the British were developing a long-term plan to reduce the colonies to a subservient position, which they were soon calling "slavery." This view was ill-informed, however. Grenville's measures had been designed as a carefully considered package; apart from some tidying-up legislation, Grenville had had no further plans for the colonies after the Stamp Act. His successors developed further measures, not as extensions of an original plan but because the Stamp Act had been repealed.

Nevertheless, the colonists were outraged. In Pennsylvania the lawyer and legislator John Dickinson wrote a series of essays that, appearing in 1767 and 1768 as *Letters from a Farmer* in Pennsylvania, were widely reprinted and exerted great influence in forming a united colonial opposition. Dickinson agreed that Parliament had supreme power where the whole empire was concerned, but he denied that it had power over internal colonial affairs; he quietly implied that the basis of colonial loyalty lay in its utility among equals rather than in obedience owed to a superior.

It proved easier to unite on opinion than on action. Gradually, after much maneuvering and negotiation, a wide-ranging nonimportation policy against British goods was brought into operation. Agreement had not been easy to reach, and the tensions sometimes broke out in acrimonious charges of noncooperation.

In addition, the policy had to be enforced by newly created local committees, a process that put a new disciplinary power in the hands of local men who had not had much previous experience in public affairs. There were, as a result, many signs of discontent with the ordering of domestic affairs in some of the colonies—a development that had obvious implications for the future of colonial politics if more action was needed later.

CONSTITUTIONAL DIFFERENCES WITH BRITAIN

Very few colonists wanted or even envisaged independence at this stage. (Dickinson had hinted at such a possibility with expressions of pain that were obviously sincere.) The colonial struggle for power, although charged with intense feeling, was not an attempt to change government structure but an argument over legal interpretation. The core of the colonial case was that, as British subjects, they were entitled to the same privileges as their fellow subjects in Britain. They could not constitutionally be taxed without their own consent; and, because they were unrepresented in the Parliament that voted the taxes, they had not given this consent. James Otis, in two long pamphlets, ceded all sovereign power to Parliament with this proviso. Others, however, began to question whether Parliament did have lawful power to legislate over the colonies. These doubts were expressed by the late 1760s, when James Wilson, a Scottish immigrant lawyer living in Philadelphia, wrote an essay on the subject. Because of the withdrawal of the Townshend round of duties in 1770, Wilson kept this essay private until new troubles arose in 1774, when he published it as *Considerations on the Nature and Extent of the Legislative Authority of the British Parliament.* In this he fully articulated a view that had been gathering force in the colonies (it was also the opinion of Franklin) that Parliament's lawful sovereignty stopped at the shores of Britain.

The official British reply to the colonial case on representation was that the colonies were "virtually" represented in Parliament in the same sense that the large voteless majority of the British public was represented by those who did vote. To this Otis snorted that, if the majority of the British people did not have the vote, they ought to have it. The idea of colonial members of Parliament, several times suggested, was never a likely solution because of problems of time and distance and because, from the colonists' point of view, colonial members would not have adequate influence.

The standpoints of the two sides to the controversy could be traced in the language used. The principle of parliamentary sovereignty was expressed in the language of paternalistic authority; the British referred to themselves as parents and to the colonists as children. Colonial Tories, who accepted Parliament's case in the interests of social stability, also used this terminology. From this point of view, colonial insubordination was "unnatural," just as the revolt of children against parents was unnatural. The colonists replied to all this in the language of rights. They held that Parliament could do nothing in the colonies that it could not do in Britain because the Americans were protected by all the common-law rights of the British. (When the First Continental Congress met in September 1774, one of its first acts was to affirm that the colonies were entitled to the common law of England.)

Rights, as Richard Bland of Virginia insisted in *The Colonel Dismounted* (as early as 1764), implied equality. And

JAMES OTIS

James Otis (Feb. 5, 1725–May 23, 1783) was an American political activist during the period leading up to the American Revolution. He helped formulate the colonists' grievances against the British government in the 1760s.

Son of the elder James Otis, who was already prominent in Massachusetts politics, the younger Otis graduated from Harvard College in 1743 and was admitted to the bar in 1748. He moved his law practice from Plymouth to Boston in 1750. His reputation was built mainly upon his famous challenge in 1761 to the British-imposed writs of assistance—general search warrants designed to enforce more strictly the trade and navigation laws in North America. These search warrants authorized customhouse officers to search any house for smuggled goods; neither the house nor the goods had to be specifically mentioned in the writs. Arguing before the Superior Court in Boston, Otis raised the doctrine of natural law underlying the rights of citizens and argued that such writs, even if authorized by Parliament, were null and void. In harking back to fundamental English constitutional law, Otis offered the colonists a basic doctrine upon which their publicists could draw for decades to come. At this time he also reportedly coined the oft-quoted phrase "Taxation without representation is tyranny."

Otis was elected in May 1761 to the General Court (provincial legislature) of Massachusetts and was reelected nearly every year thereafter during his active life. In 1766 he was chosen speaker of the house, though this choice was negated by the royal governor of the province.

In September 1762 Otis published *A Vindication of the Conduct of the House of Representatives of the Province of Massachusetts Bay* in defense of that body's rebuke of the governor for asking the assembly to pay for ships not authorized by them—though sent to protect New England fisheries against French privateers. Otis also wrote various state papers addressed to the colonies to enlist them in the common cause, and he also sent such papers to the government in England to uphold the rights or set forth the grievances of the colonists. His influence at home in controlling and directing the movement of events toward freedom was universally felt and acknowledged, and few Americans were so frequently quoted, denounced, or applauded in Parliament and the British press before 1769. In 1765 he was a delegate to the Stamp Act Congress in New York City, and there he was a conspicuous figure, serving on the committee that prepared the address sent to the House of Commons.

Already prone to fits of insanity, Otis was struck on the head during an altercation with a crown officer in 1769 and was rendered harmlessly insane, with only occasional lucid intervals, until his death. He died in 1783 after being struck by lightning.

here he touched on the underlying source of colonial grievance. Americans were being treated as unequals, which they not only resented but also feared would lead to a loss of control of their own affairs. Colonists perceived legal inequality when writs of assistance—essentially, general search warrants—were authorized in Boston in 1761 while closely related "general warrants" were outlawed in two celebrated cases in Britain. Townshend specifically legalized writs of assistance in the colonies in 1767. Dickinson devoted one of his *Letters from a Farmer* to this issue.

When Lord North became prime minister early in 1770, George III had at last found a minister who could work both with himself and with Parliament. British government began to acquire some stability. In 1770, in the face of the American policy of nonimportation, the Townshend tariffs were withdrawn—all except the tax on tea, which was kept for symbolic reasons. Relative calm returned, though it was ruffled on the New England coastline by frequent incidents of defiance of customs officers, who could get no support from local juries. These outbreaks did not win much sympathy from other colonies, but they were serious enough to call for an increase in the number of British regular forces stationed in Boston. One of the most violent clashes occurred in Boston just before the repeal of the Townshend duties. Threatened by mob harassment, a small British detachment opened fire and killed five people, an incident soon known as the Boston Massacre. The soldiers were charged with murder and were given a civilian trial, in which John Adams conducted a successful defense.

The other serious quarrel with British authority occurred in New York, where the assembly refused to accept all the British demands for quartering troops. Before a compromise was reached, Parliament had threatened to suspend the assembly. The episode was ominous because it indicated that Parliament was taking the Declaratory Act at its word; on no previous occasion had the British legislature intervened in the operation of the constitution in an American colony. (Such interventions, which were rare, had come from the crown.)

British intervention in colonial economic affairs occurred again when in 1773 Lord North's administration tried to rescue the East India Company from difficulties that had nothing to do with America. The Tea Act gave the company, which produced tea in India, a monopoly of distribution in the colonies. The company planned to sell its tea through its own agents, eliminating the system of sale by auction to independent merchants. By thus cutting the costs of middlemen, it hoped to undersell the widely purchased inferior smuggled tea. This plan naturally affected colonial merchants, and many colonists denounced the act as a plot to induce Americans to buy—and therefore pay the tax on—legally imported tea. Boston was not the only port to threaten to reject the casks of taxed tea, but its reply was the most dramatic—and provocative.

On Dec. 16, 1773, a party of Bostonians, thinly disguised as Mohawk Indians, boarded the ships at anchor and dumped some £10,000 worth of tea into the harbour, an event popularly known as the Boston Tea Party. British opinion was outraged, and America's friends in Parliament were immobilized. (American merchants in other cities were also disturbed. Property was property.) In the spring of 1774, with hardly any opposition, Parliament passed a series of measures designed to reduce Massachusetts to order and imperial discipline. The port of Boston was closed, and, in the Massachusetts Government Act, Parliament for the first time actually altered a colonial charter, substituting an appointive council for the elective one established in 1691 and conferring extensive powers on the governor and council. The famous town meeting, a forum for radical thinkers, was outlawed as a political body. To make matters worse, Parliament also passed the Quebec Act for the government of Canada. To the horror of pious New England Calvinists, the Roman Catholic religion was recognized for the French inhabitants. In addition, Upper Canada (i.e., the southern section) was joined to the Mississippi valley for purposes of administration, permanently blocking the prospect of American control of western settlement.

THE INTOLERABLE ACTS

Also called the Coercive Acts (1774), the Intolerable Acts were four punitive measures enacted by the British Parliament in retaliation for acts of colonial defiance, together with the Quebec Act establishing a new administration for the territory ceded to Britain after the French and Indian War (1754–63).

First, angered by the Boston Tea Party (1773), the British government passed the Boston Port Bill, closing that city's harbour until restitution was made for the destroyed tea. Second, the Massachusetts Government Act abrogated the colony's charter of 1691, reducing it to the level of a crown colony, substituting a military government under General Thomas Gage, and forbidding town meetings without approval.

The third, the Administration of Justice Act, was aimed at protecting British officials charged with capital offenses during law enforcement by allowing them to go to England or another colony for trial. The fourth Coercive Act included new arrangements for housing British troops in occupied American dwellings, thus reviving the indignation that surrounded the earlier Quartering Act, which had been allowed to expire in 1770.

The Quebec Act, under consideration since 1773, removed all the territory and fur trade between the Ohio and Mississippi rivers from possible colonial jurisdiction and awarded it to the province of Quebec. By establishing French civil law and the Roman Catholic religion in the coveted area, Britain acted liberally toward Quebec's settlers but raised the spectre of popery before the mainly Protestant colonies to Canada's south.

The Intolerable Acts represented an attempt to reimpose strict British control over the American colonies, but after 10

THE BOSTON TEA PARTY

On December 16, 1773, an incident known as the Boston Tea Party occurred. American patriots disguised as Mohawk Indians threw 342 chests of tea belonging to the British East India Company from ships into Boston Harbor. The Americans were protesting both a tax on tea (taxation without representation) and the perceived monopoly of the East India Company.

The Townshend Acts passed by Parliament in 1767 and imposing duties on various products imported into the British colonies had raised such a storm of colonial protest and noncompliance that they were repealed in 1770, saving the duty on tea, which was retained by Parliament to demonstrate its presumed right to raise such colonial revenue without colonial approval. The merchants of Boston circumvented the act by continuing to receive tea smuggled in by Dutch traders. In 1773 Parliament passed a Tea Act designed to aid the financially troubled East India Company by granting it (1) a monopoly on all tea exported to the colonies, (2) an exemption on the export tax, and (3) a "drawback" (refund) on duties owed on certain surplus quantities of tea in its possession. The tea sent to the colonies was to be carried only in East India Company ships and sold only through its own agents, bypassing the independent colonial shippers and merchants. The company thus could sell the tea at a less-than-usual price in either America or Britain; it could undersell anyone else. The perception of monopoly drove the normally conservative colonial merchants into an alliance with radicals led by Samuel Adams and his Sons of Liberty.

In such cities as New York, Philadelphia, and Charleston, tea agents resigned or canceled orders, and merchants refused consignments. In Boston, however, the royal governor Thomas

(*continued on the next page*)

THE BOSTON TEA PARTY (CONTINUED)

Hutchinson determined to uphold the law and maintained that three arriving ships, the Dartmouth, Eleanor, and Beaver, should be allowed to deposit their cargoes and that appropriate duties should be honoured. On the night of December 16, 1773, a group of about 60 men, encouraged by a large crowd of Bostonians, donned blankets and Indian headdresses, marched to Griffin's wharf, boarded the ships, and dumped the tea chests, valued at £18,000, into the water.

In retaliation, Parliament passed the series of punitive measures known in the colonies as the Intolerable Acts, including the Boston Port Bill, which shut off the city's sea trade pending payment for the destroyed tea. The British government's efforts to single out Massachusetts for punishment served only to unite the colonies and impel the drift toward war.

years of vacillation, the decision to be firm had come too late. Rather than cowing Massachusetts and separating it from the other colonies, the oppressive measures became the justification for convening the First Continental Congress later in 1774.

THE CONTINENTAL CONGRESS

There was widespread agreement that this intervention in colonial government could threaten other provinces and could be countered only by collective action. After much intercolonial correspondence, a Continental Congress came into existence, meeting in Philadelphia in September 1774. Every colonial assembly except that of Georgia appointed and sent a delegation. The Virginia delegation's instructions were drafted by Thomas Jefferson and were later published as *A Summary View of the Rights of British America* (1774). Jefferson insisted on the autonomy of colonial legislative power and set forth a highly individualistic view of the basis of American rights. This belief that the American colonies and other members of the British Empire were distinct states united under the king and thus subject only to the king and not to Parliament was shared by several other delegates, notably James Wilson and John Adams, and strongly influenced the Congress.

The Congress's first important decision was one on procedure: whether to vote by colony, each having one vote, or by wealth calculated on a ratio with population. The decision to vote by colony was made on practical grounds—neither wealth nor population could be satisfactorily ascertained—but it had important consequences. Individual colonies, no matter what their size, retained a degree of autonomy that translated immediately into the language and prerogatives of sovereignty. Under Massachusetts's influence, the Congress next adopted the Suffolk Resolves, recently voted in Suffolk county, Mass., which for the first time put natural rights into the official colonial argument (hitherto all remonstrances had been based on common law and constitutional rights). Apart from this, however, the prevailing mood was cautious.

The Congress's aim was to put such pressure on the British government that it would redress all colonial grievances and restore the harmony that had once prevailed. The Congress thus adopted an association that committed the colonies to a carefully phased plan of economic pressure, beginning with nonimportation, moving to nonconsumption, and finishing the following September (after the rice harvest had been exported) with nonexportation. A few New England and Virginia delegates were looking toward independence, but the majority went home hoping that these steps, together with new appeals to the king and to the British people, would avert the need for any further such meetings. If these measures failed, however, a second Congress would convene the following spring.

Behind the unity achieved by the Congress lay deep divisions in colonial society. In the mid-1760s upriver New York was disrupted by land riots, which also broke out in parts of New Jersey; much worse disorder ravaged the backcountry of both North and South Carolina, where frontier people were left unprotected by legislatures that taxed them but in which they felt themselves unrepresented. A pitched battle at Alamance Creek in North Carolina in 1771 ended that rising, known as the Regulator Insurrection, and was followed by executions for treason. Although without such serious disorder, the cities also revealed acute social tensions and resentments of inequalities of economic opportunity and visible status. New York provincial politics were riven by intense rivalry between two great family-based factions, the DeLanceys, who benefited from royal government connections, and their rivals, the Livingstons. (The politics of the quarrel with Britain affected the domestic standing of these groups and eventually eclipsed the DeLanceys.) Another phenomenon was the rapid rise of dissenting religious sects, notably the Baptists; although they carried no political program, their style of preaching suggested a strong undercurrent of social as well as religious dissent. There was no inherent unity to these disturbances, but many leaders of colonial society were reluctant to ally themselves with these disruptive elements even in protest against Britain. They were concerned about the domestic consequences of letting the protests take a revolutionary turn; power shared with these elements might never be recovered.

In the spring of 1774 the British Parliament's passage of the Intolerable (Coercive) Acts, including the closing of the port of Boston, provoked keen resentment in the colonies. The First Continental Congress, convened in response to the Acts by the colonial Committees of Correspondence, met in Philadelphia on September 5, 1774. Fifty-six deputies represented all the colonies except Georgia. Peyton Randolph of Virginia was unanimously elected president, thus establishing usage of that term as well as "Congress." Charles Thomson of Pennsylvania was elected secretary and served in that office during the 15-year life of the Congress.

When British Gen. Thomas Gage sent a force from Boston to destroy American rebel military stores at Concord, Mass., fighting broke out between militia and British troops at Lexington and Concord on April 19, 1775. Reports of these clashes reached the Second Continental Congress, which met in Philadelphia in May. Although most colonial leaders still hoped for reconciliation with Britain, the news stirred the delegates to more radical action. Steps were taken to put the continent on a war footing. While a further appeal was addressed to the British people (mainly at Dickinson's insistence), the Congress raised an army, adopted a Declaration of the Causes and Necessity of Taking Up Arms, and appointed committees to deal with domestic supply and foreign affairs. In August 1775 the king declared a state of rebellion; by the end of the year, all colonial trade had been banned. Even yet, Gen. George Washington, commander of the Continental Army, still referred to the

BRITISH SHIPS GUARD BOSTON HARBOUR IN 1774. ONE OF THE INTOLERABLE ACTS, PASSED BY PARLIAMENT THAT YEAR, CLOSED THE HARBOUR TO PUNISH AMERICAN COLONISTS FOR ACTS OF DEFIANCE.

British troops as "ministerial" forces, indicating a civil war, not a war looking to separate national identity.

Then in January 1776 the publication of Thomas Paine's irreverent pamphlet *Common Sense* abruptly shattered this hopeful complacency and put independence on the agenda. Paine's eloquent, direct language spoke people's unspoken thoughts; no pamphlet had ever made such an impact on colonial opinion. While the Congress negotiated urgently, but secretly, for a French alliance, power struggles erupted in provinces where conservatives still hoped for relief. The only form relief could take, however,

ALTHOUGH IN AUGUST 1775 GREAT BRITAIN'S KING GEORGE III ANNOUNCED A STATE OF REBELLION AND LATER BANNED ALL COLONIAL TRADE, MOST COLONISTS HOPED TO AVOID A CIVIL WAR.

was British concessions; as public opinion hardened in Britain, where a general election in November 1774 had returned a strong majority for Lord North, the hope for reconciliation faded. In the face of British intransigence, men committed to their definition of colonial rights were left with no alternative, and the substantial portion of colonists—about one-third according to John Adams, although contemporary historians believe the number to have been much smaller—who preferred loyalty to the crown, with all its disadvantages, were localized and outflanked. Where the British armies massed, they found plenty of loyalist support, but, when they moved on, they left the loyalists feeble and exposed.

The most dramatic internal revolution occurred in Pennsylvania, where a strong radical party, based mainly in Philadelphia but with allies in the country, seized power in the course of the controversy over independence itself. Opinion for independence swept the colonies in the spring of 1776. The Congress recommended that colonies form their own governments and assigned a committee to draft a declaration of independence.

This document, written by Thomas Jefferson but revised in committee, consisted of two parts. The preamble set the claims of the United States on a basis of natural rights, with a dedication to the principle of equality; the second was a long list of grievances against the crown—not Parliament now, since the argument was that Parliament had no lawful power in the colonies. On July 2 the Congress itself voted for independence; on July 4 it adopted the Declaration of Independence.

REVOLUTION!

The American Revolutionary War thus began as a civil conflict within the British Empire over colonial affairs, but, with America being joined by France in 1778, Spain in 1779, and the Netherlands in 1780, it became an international war. On land the Americans assembled both state militias and the Continental (national) Army, with approximately 20,000 men, mostly farmers, fighting at any given time. By contrast, the British army was composed of reliable and well-trained professionals, numbering about 42,000 regulars, supplemented by about 30,000 German (Hessian) mercenaries.

After the fighting at Lexington and Concord that began the war, rebel forces began a siege of Boston that ended when the American Gen. Henry Knox arrived with artillery captured from Fort Ticonderoga, forcing Gen. William Howe, Gage's replacement, to evacuate Boston on March 17, 1776. An American force under Gen. Richard Montgomery invaded Canada in the fall of 1775, captured Montreal, and launched an unsuccessful attack on Quebec, in which Montgomery was killed. The Americans maintained a siege on the city until the arrival of British reinforcements in the spring and then retreated to Fort Ticonderoga.

The British government sent Howe's brother, Richard, Adm. Lord Howe, with a large fleet to join his brother in New York, authorizing them to treat with the Americans and assure them pardon should they submit. When the Americans refused this offer of peace, General Howe landed on Long Island and on August 27 defeated the army led by Washington, who retreated into Manhattan. Howe drew him north, defeated his army at Chatterton Hill near White Plains on October 28, and then stormed the garrison Washington had left behind on Manhattan, seizing prisoners and supplies. Lord Charles Cornwallis, having taken Washington's other garrison at Fort Lee, drove the American army across New Jersey to the western bank of the Delaware River and then quartered his troops for the winter at outposts in New Jersey. On Christmas night Washington stealthily crossed the Delaware and attacked Cornwallis's garrison at Trenton, taking nearly 1,000 prisoners. Though Cornwallis soon recaptured Trenton, Washington escaped and

On October 17, 1777, after dual defeats by American forces, British Gen. John Burgoyne's quest to reach Albany, N.Y., was thwarted once and for all. He surrendered at Saratoga.

BATTLES OF TRENTON AND PRINCETON

The battles of Trenton and Princeton (1776–77), in the American Revolution, are notable as the first successes won by the Revolutionary general George Washington in the open field. After the capture of Fort Washington on Manhattan Island in November 1776, the British general Sir William Howe forced the Americans to retreat through New Jersey and across the Delaware River into Pennsylvania. Howe then went into winter quarters, leaving the Hessian colonel Johann Rall at Trenton with about 1,400 men.

Although Washington's Continental Army was discouraged by the year's disasters, its morale was not crushed, and it now numbered 6,000 effectives. Ascertaining that the Hessians were virtually unsupported, Washington determined to attempt their capture. Despite the ice floes in the Delaware, Washington crossed the river on December 25 and surprised the enemy, the next day capturing more than 900 men. Four days later he occupied Trenton. Hearing of Washington's move, Lord Cornwallis confronted the Continentals east of the city with about 7,000 troops on January 2, 1777, driving them back. Unable to find boats for an escape, Washington called a council of war that confirmed his bold plan to break camp quietly that night and take a byroad to Princeton. The maneuver succeeded, and three British regiments that met him there on January 3 were all driven back or retreated. As a result, Washington continued his march to Morristown, New Jersey, where he flanked British communications with New York. Cornwallis retired to New Brunswick. Besides succeeding in breaking through Howe's lines, Washington had placed himself in an advantageous position for recruiting his army and maintaining a strong defensive in the next campaign.

The effect of these early American victories in the battles of Trenton and Princeton was marked. Following close upon a series of defeats, they put new life into the American cause and renewed confidence in Washington as commander of the Revolutionary army.

went on to defeat British reinforcements at Princeton. Washington's Trenton-Princeton campaign roused the new country and kept the struggle for independence alive.

In 1777 a British army under Gen. John Burgoyne moved south from Canada with Albany, N.Y., as its goal. Burgoyne captured Fort Ticonderoga on July 5, but, as he approached Albany, he was twice defeated by an American force led by Generals Horatio Gates and Benedict Arnold, and on Oct. 17, 1777, at Saratoga, he was forced to surrender his army. Earlier that fall Howe had sailed from New York to Chesapeake Bay, and once ashore he had defeated Washington's forces at Brandywine Creek on September 11 and occupied the American capital of Philadelphia on September 25.

After a mildly successful attack at Germantown, Pa., on October 4, Washington quartered his 11,000 troops for the winter at Valley Forge, Pa. Though the conditions at Valley Forge were bleak and food was scarce, a Prussian officer, Baron Friedrich Wilhelm von Steuben, was able to give the American troops valuable training in maneuvers and in the more efficient use of their weapons. Von Steuben's aid contributed greatly to Washington's success at Monmouth (now Freehold), N.J., on June 28, 1778. After that battle British forces in the north remained chiefly in and around the city of New York.

AT WAR ON LAND AND SEA

The American Revolution (1775–83) followed more than a decade of growing estrangement between the British crown and a large and influential segment of its North American colonies that was caused by British attempts to assert greater control over colonial affairs. Until early in 1778 the conflict was a civil war within the British Empire; afterward it became an international war as France (in 1778), Spain (in 1779), and the Netherlands (in 1780) joined the colonies against Britain. From the beginning sea power was vital in determining the course of the war, lending to British strategy a flexibility that helped compensate for the comparatively small numbers of troops sent to America and ultimately enabling the French to help bring about the final British surrender at Yorktown.

LAND CAMPAIGNS TO 1778

Americans fought the war on land essentially with two types of organization, the Continental (national) Army and the state militias. The total number of the former provided by quotas from the states throughout the conflict was 231,771 men; the militias totaled 164,087. At any given time, however, the American forces seldom numbered more than 20,000; in 1781 there were only about 29,000 insurgents under arms throughout the country. The war was therefore one fought by small field armies. Militias, poorly disciplined and with elected officers, were summoned for periods usually not exceeding three months. The terms of Continental Army service were only gradually increased from one to three years, and not even bounties and the offer of land kept the army up to strength. Reasons for the difficulty in maintaining an adequate Continental force included the colonists' traditional antipathy to regular armies, the objections of farmers to being away from their fields, the competition of the states with the Continental Congress to keep men in the militia, and the wretched and uncertain pay in a period of inflation.

By contrast, the British army was a reliable, steady force of professionals. Because it numbered only about 42,000, heavy recruiting programs were introduced. Many of the enlisted

IN SPITE OF SCANT SUPPLIES DURING THE LONG, STARK WINTER OF 1777, GEORGE WASHINGTON AND HIS TROOPS TRAINED, LEARNING IMPORTANT DRILLS AND IMPROVING THEIR USE OF WEAPONS AT VALLEY FORGE, PA.

men were farm boys, as were most of the Americans. Others were unemployed persons from the urban slums. Still others joined the army to escape fines or imprisonment. The great majority became efficient soldiers owing to sound training and ferocious discipline. The officers were drawn largely from the gentry and the aristocracy and obtained their commissions and promotions by purchase. Though they received no formal training, they were not so dependent on a book knowledge of military tactics as were many of the Americans. British generals, however, tended toward a lack of imagination and initiative, while those who demonstrated such qualities often were rash.

Because troops were few and conscription unknown, the British government, following a traditional policy, purchased about 30,000 troops from various German princes. The Landgrave of Hesse furnished approximately three-fifths of this total. Few acts by the crown roused so much antagonism in America as this use of foreign mercenaries.

The war began in Massachusetts when General Thomas Gage sent a force from Boston to destroy rebel military stores at Concord. Fighting occurred at Lexington and Concord on April 19, 1775, and only the arrival of reinforcements saved the British original column. Rebel militia then converged on Boston from all over New England. Their entrenching on Breed's Hill led to a British frontal assault on June 17 under General William Howe, who won the hill but at the cost of more than 40 percent of the assault force.

General George Washington was appointed commander in chief of the American forces by the Continental Congress. Not only did he have to contain the British in Boston but he had also to recruit a continental army. During the winter of 1775–76, recruitment lagged so badly that fresh drafts of militia

A line of minutemen are fired upon by British troops during the Battle of Lexington in Massachusetts, April 19, 1775.

were called up to help maintain the siege. The balance shifted in late winter, when General Henry Knox arrived with artillery from Fort Ticonderoga in New York, which had been captured from the British in May 1775. Mounted on Dorchester Heights, above Boston, the guns forced Howe, who had replaced Gage in command, to evacuate the city on March 17, 1776. Howe then repaired to Halifax to prepare for an invasion of New York, and Washington moved units southward for its defense.

Meanwhile, action flared in the north. In the fall of 1775 the Americans invaded Canada. One force under General Richard

Montgomery captured Montreal on November 13. Another under Benedict Arnold made a remarkable march through the Maine wilderness to Quebec. Unable to take the city, Arnold was presently joined by Montgomery, many of whose troops had gone home because their enlistments had expired. An attack on the city on the last day of the year failed, Montgomery was killed, and many troops were captured. The Americans maintained a siege of the city but withdrew with the arrival of British reinforcements in the spring. Pursued by the British and decimated by smallpox, the Americans fell back to Ticonderoga. General Guy Carleton's hopes of moving quickly down Lake Champlain, however, were frustrated by Arnold's construction of a fighting fleet. Forced to build one of his own, Carleton destroyed most of the American fleet in October 1776 but considered the season too advanced to bring Ticonderoga under siege.

As the Americans suffered defeat in Canada, so did the British in the South. North Carolina patriots trounced a body of loyalists at Moore's Creek Bridge on February 27, 1776. Charleston, South Carolina, was successfully defended against a British assault by sea in June.

Having made up its mind to crush the rebellion, the British government sent General Howe and his brother, Richard, Admiral Lord Howe, with a large fleet and 34,000 British and German troops to New York. It also gave the Howes a commission to treat with the Americans. The Continental Congress, which had proclaimed the independence of the colonies, at first thought the Howes empowered to negotiate peace terms but discovered that they were authorized only to accept submission and assure pardons.

Their peace efforts getting nowhere, the Howes turned to force. Under his brother's guns, General Howe landed troops on Long Island and on August 27 scored a smashing victory. Washington evacuated his army from Brooklyn to Manhattan that night under cover of a fog. On September 15 Howe followed up his victory by invading Manhattan. Though checked at Harlem Heights the next day, he drew Washington off the island in October by a move to Throg's Neck and then to New Rochelle, northeast of the city. Leaving garrisons at Fort Washington on Manhattan and at Fort Lee on the opposite shore of the Hudson River, Washington hastened to block Howe. The latter, however, defeated him on October 28 at Chatterton Hill near White Plains. Howe slipped between the American army and Fort Washington and stormed the fort on November 16, seizing nearly 3,000 prisoners, guns, and supplies. British forces under Lord Cornwallis then took Fort Lee and on November 24 started to drive the American army across New Jersey. Though Washington escaped to the west bank of the Delaware River, his army nearly disappeared. Howe then put his army into winter quarters, with outposts at towns such as Bordentown and Trenton.

On Christmas night Washington struck back with a brilliant riposte. Crossing the ice-strewn Delaware with 2,400 men, he fell upon the Hessian garrison at Trenton at dawn and took nearly 1,000 prisoners. Though almost trapped by Cornwallis, who recovered Trenton on January 2, 1777, Washington made a skillful escape during the night, won a battle against British reinforcements at Princeton the next day, and went into winter quarters in the defensible area around Morristown. The Trenton-Princeton campaign roused the country and saved the struggle for independence from collapse.

Britain's strategy in 1777 aimed at driving a wedge between New England and the other colonies. An army under General John Burgoyne was to march south from Canada and join forces with Howe on the Hudson. But Howe seems to have concluded that Burgoyne was strong enough to operate on his own and left New York in the summer, taking his army by sea to the head of Chesapeake Bay. Once ashore, he defeated Washington badly but not decisively at Brandywine Creek on September 11. Then, feinting westward, he entered Philadelphia, the American capital, on September 25. The Continental Congress fled to York. Washington struck back at Germantown on October 4 but, compelled to withdraw, went into winter quarters at Valley Forge.

In the north the story was different. Burgoyne was to move south to Albany with a force of about 9,000 British, Germans, Indians, and American loyalists; a smaller force under Lieutenant Colonel Barry St. Leger was to converge on Albany through the Mohawk valley. Burgoyne took Ticonderoga handily on July 5 and then, instead of using Lake George, chose a southward route by land. Slowed by the rugged terrain, strewn with trees cut down by American axmen under General Philip Schuyler, and needing horses, Burgoyne sent a force of Germans to collect them at Bennington, Vermont. The Germans were nearly wiped out on August 16 by New Englanders under General John Stark and Colonel Seth Warner. Meanwhile, St. Leger besieged Fort Schuyler (present Rome, New York), ambushed a relief column of American militia at Oriskany on August 6, but retreated as his Indians gave up the siege and an American force under Arnold approached. Burgoyne himself reached the Hudson, but the Americans, now under General Horatio Gates, checked him at Freeman's Farm on September 19 and, thanks to Arnold's battlefield leadership, decisively defeated him at Bemis Heights on October 7. Ten days later, unable to get help from New York, Burgoyne surrendered at Saratoga.

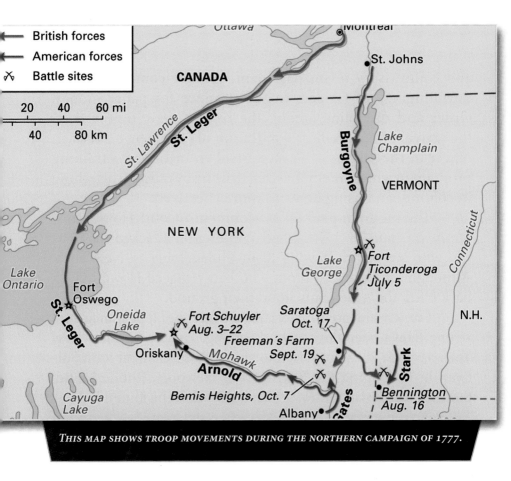

THIS MAP SHOWS TROOP MOVEMENTS DURING THE NORTHERN CAMPAIGN OF 1777.

The most significant result of Burgoyne's capitulation was the entrance of France into the war. The French had secretly furnished financial and material aid since 1776. Now they prepared fleets and armies, although they did not formally declare war until June 1778.

LAND CAMPAIGNS FROM 1778

Meanwhile, the Americans at Valley Forge survived a hungry winter, which was made worse by quartermaster

35

and commissary mismanagement, graft of contractors, and unwillingness of farmers to sell produce for paper money. Order and discipline among the troops were improved by the arrival of the Freiherr von (baron of) Steuben, a Prussian officer in the service of France. Steuben instituted a training program in which he emphasized drilling by officers, marching in column, and using firearms more effectively.

The program paid off at Monmouth Court House, New Jersey, on June 28, 1778, when Washington attacked the British, who were withdrawing from Philadelphia to New York. Although Sir Henry Clinton, who had replaced Howe, struck back hard, the Americans stood their ground.

French aid now materialized with the appearance of a strong fleet under the comte d'Estaing. Unable to enter New York harbour, d'Estaing tried to assist Major General John Sullivan in dislodging the British from Newport, Rhode Island. Storms and British reinforcements thwarted the joint effort.

Action in the North was largely a stalemate for the rest of the war. The British raided New Bedford, Massachusetts, and New Haven and New London, Connecticut, while loyalists and Indians attacked settlements in New York and Pennsylvania. On the other hand, the Americans under Anthony Wayne stormed Stony Point, New York, on July 16, 1779, and "Light-Horse Harry" Lee took Paulus Hook, New Jersey, on August 19. More lasting in effect was Sullivan's expedition of August 1779 against Britain's Indian allies in New York, particularly the destruction of their villages and fields of corn. Farther west, Colonel George Rogers Clark seized Vincennes and other posts north of the Ohio River in 1778.

Potentially serious blows to the American cause were Arnold's defection in 1780 and the army mutinies of 1780 and

1781. Arnold's attempt to betray West Point to the British miscarried. Mutinies were sparked by misunderstandings over terms of enlistment, poor food and clothing, gross arrears of pay, and the decline in the purchasing power of the dollar. Suppressed by force or negotiation, the mutinies shook the morale of the army.

The Americans also suffered setbacks in the South. British strategy from 1778 called for offensives that were designed to take advantage of the flexibility of sea power and the loyalist sentiment of many of the people. British forces from New York and St. Augustine, Florida, occupied Georgia by the end of January 1779 and successfully defended Savannah in the fall against d'Estaing and a Franco-American army. Clinton, having withdrawn his Newport garrison, captured Charleston—and an American army of 5,000 under General Benjamin Lincoln—in May 1780. Learning that Newport was threatened by a French expeditionary force under the comte de Rochambeau, Clinton returned to New York, leaving Cornwallis at Charleston.

Cornwallis, however, took the offensive. On August 16 he shattered General Gates's army at Camden, South Carolina. The destruction of a force of loyalists at Kings Mountain on October 7 led him to move against the new American commander, General Nathanael Greene. When Greene put part of his force under General Daniel Morgan, Cornwallis sent his cavalry leader, Colonel Banastre Tarleton, after Morgan. At Cowpens on January 17, 1781, Morgan destroyed practically all of Tarleton's column. Subsequently, on March 15, Greene and Cornwallis fought at Guilford Courthouse, North Carolina. Cornwallis won but suffered heavy casualties. After withdrawing to Wilmington, he marched into Virginia to join British forces sent there by Clinton.

Greene then moved back to South Carolina, where he was defeated by Lord Rawdon at Hobkirk's Hill on April 25 and at Ninety-Six in June and by Lieutenant Colonel Alexander Stewart at Eutaw Springs on September 8. In spite of this, the British, harassed by partisan leaders such as Francis Marion, Thomas Sumter, and Andrew Pickens, soon retired to the coast and remained locked up in Charleston and Savannah.

Meanwhile, Cornwallis entered Virginia. Sending Tarleton on raids across the state, he started to build a base at Yorktown, at the same time fending off American forces under Wayne, Steuben, and the marquis de Lafayette.

Learning that the comte de Grasse had arrived in the Chesapeake with a large fleet and 3,000 French troops, Washington and Rochambeau moved south to Virginia. By mid-September the Franco-American forces had placed Yorktown under siege, and British rescue efforts proved fruitless. Cornwallis surrendered his army of more than 7,000 men on October 19. Thus, for the second time during the war the British had lost an entire army.

Thereafter, land action in America died out, though the war persisted in other theatres and on the high seas. Eventually Clinton was replaced by Sir Guy Carleton. While the peace treaties were under consideration and afterward, Carleton evacuated thousands of loyalists from America, including many from Savannah on July 11, 1782, and others from Charleston on December 14. The last British forces finally left New York on November 25, 1783. Washington then reentered the city in triumph.

THE WAR AT SEA

Although the colonists ventured to challenge Britain's naval power from the outbreak of the conflict, the war at sea in its later stages was fought mainly between Britain and America's European allies, the American effort being reduced to privateering.

The importance of sea power was recognized early. In October 1775 the Continental Congress authorized the creation of the Continental Navy and established the Marine Corps in November. The navy, taking its direction from the naval and marine committees of the Congress, was only occasionally effective. In 1776 it had 27 ships against Britain's 270; by the end of the war, the British total had risen close to 500, and the American had dwindled to 20. Many of the best seamen available went off privateering, and both Continental Navy commanders and crews suffered from a lack of training and discipline.

The first significant blow by the navy was struck by Commodore Esek Hopkins, who captured New Providence (Nassau) in the Bahamas in 1776. Other captains, such as Lambert Wickes, Gustavus Conyngham, and John Barry, also enjoyed successes, but the Scottish-born John Paul Jones was especially notable. As captain of the *Ranger*, Jones scourged the British coasts in 1778, capturing the man-of-war *Drake*. As captain of the *Bonhomme Richard* in 1779, he intercepted a timber convoy and captured the British frigate *Serapis*.

More injurious to the British were the raids by American privateers on their shipping. American ships, furnished with letters of marque by the Congress or the states, swarmed about the British Isles. By the end of 1777 they had taken 560 British vessels, and by the end of the war they had probably seized 1,500. More than 12,000 British sailors also were captured. One result was that, by 1781, British merchants were clamouring for an end to hostilities.

Most of the naval action occurred at sea. The significant exceptions were Arnold's battles against General Carleton's

In 1779, Captain John Paul Jones and the crew of the Bonhomme Richard battled it out with and ultimately apprehended a British warship.

fleet on Lake Champlain at Valcour Island on October 11 and off Split Rock on October 13, 1776. Arnold lost both battles, but his construction of a fleet of tiny vessels, mostly gondolas (gundalows) and galleys, had forced the British to build a larger fleet and hence delayed their attack on Fort Ticonderoga until the following spring. This delay contributed significantly to Burgoyne's capitulation in October 1777.

The entrance of France into the war, followed by that of Spain in 1779 and the Netherlands in 1780, effected important changes in the naval aspect of the war. The Spanish and Dutch were not particularly active, but their role in keeping British naval forces tied down in Europe was significant. The British navy could not maintain an effective blockade of both the American coast and the enemies' ports. Owing to years of economy and neglect, Britain's ships of the line were neither modern nor sufficiently numerous. An immediate result was that France's Toulon fleet under d'Estaing got safely away to America, where it appeared off New York and later assisted General Sullivan in the unsuccessful siege of Newport. A fierce battle off Ushant, France, in July 1778 between the Channel fleet under Admiral Augustus Keppel and the Brest fleet under the comte d'Orvilliers proved inconclusive. Had Keppel won decisively, French aid to the Americans would have diminished and Rochambeau might never have been able to lead his expedition to America.

In the following year England was in real danger. Not only did it have to face the privateers of the United States, France, and Spain off its coasts, as well as the raids of John Paul Jones, but it also lived in fear of invasion. The combined fleets of France and Spain had acquired command of the Channel, and a French army of 50,000 waited for the propitious moment to board their transports. Luckily for the British, storms, sickness among the allied crews, and changes of plans terminated the threat.

Despite allied supremacy in the Channel in 1779, the threat of invasion, and the loss of islands in the West Indies, the British maintained control of the North American seaboard for most of 1779 and 1780, which made possible their southern land campaigns. They also reinforced Gibraltar, which the Spaniards had brought under siege in the fall of 1779, and sent a fleet under Admiral Sir George Rodney to the West Indies in early 1780. After fruitless maneuvering against the comte de Guichen, who had replaced d'Estaing, Rodney sailed for New York.

While Rodney had been in the West Indies, a French squadron slipped out of Brest and sailed to Newport with Rochambeau's army. Rodney, instead of trying to block the approach to Newport, returned to the West Indies, where, upon receiving instructions to attack Dutch possessions, he seized Sint Eustatius, the Dutch island that served as the principal depot for war materials shipped from Europe and transshipped into American vessels. He became so involved in the disposal of the enormous booty that he dallied at the island for six months.

In the meantime, a powerful British fleet relieved Gibraltar in 1781, but the price was the departure of the French fleet at Brest, part of it to India, the larger part under Admiral de Grasse to the West Indies. After maneuvering indecisively against Rodney, de Grasse received a request from Washington and Rochambeau to come to New York or the Chesapeake.

Earlier, in March, a French squadron had tried to bring troops from Newport to the Chesapeake but was forced to return by Admiral Marriot Arbuthnot, who had succeeded Lord Howe. Soon afterward Arbuthnot was replaced by Thomas Graves, a conventional-minded admiral.

Informed that a French squadron would shortly leave the West Indies, Rodney sent Samuel Hood north with a powerful force while he sailed for England, taking with him several formidable ships that might better have been left with Hood.

Soon after Hood dropped anchor in New York, de Grasse appeared in the Chesapeake, where he landed troops to help Lafayette contain Cornwallis until Washington and Rochambeau could arrive. Fearful that the comte de Barras, who was carrying Rochambeau's artillery train from Newport, might join de Grasse, and hoping to intercept him, Graves sailed with Hood to the Chesapeake. Graves had 19 ships of the line against de Grasse's 24. Though the battle that began on September 5 off the Virginia capes was not a skillfully managed affair, Graves had the worst of it and retired to New York. He ventured out again on October 17 with a strong contingent of troops and 25 ships of the line, while de Grasse, reinforced by Barras, now had 36 ships of the line. No battle occurred, however, when Graves learned that Cornwallis had surrendered.

Although Britain subsequently recouped some of its fortunes, by Rodney defeating and capturing de Grasse in the Battle of the Saints off Dominica in 1782 and British land and sea forces inflicting defeats in India, the turn of events did not significantly alter the situation in America as it existed after Yorktown. A new government under Lord Shelburne tried to get the American commissioners to agree to a separate peace, but, ultimately, the treaty negotiated with the Americans was not to go into effect until the formal conclusion of a peace with their European allies.

CHAPTER 3

FORGING PEACE AND A NEW AMERICAN NATION

The Peace of Paris (September 3, 1783) ended the U.S. War of Independence. Great Britain recognized the independence of the United States (with western boundaries to the Mississippi River) and ceded Florida to Spain.

In explaining the outcome of the war, scholars have pointed out that the British never contrived an overall general strategy for winning it. Also, even if the war could have been terminated by British power in the early stages, the generals during that period, notably Howe, declined to make a prompt, vigorous, intelligent application of that power. They acted, to be sure, within the conventions of their age, but in choosing to take minimal risks (for example, Carleton at Ticonderoga and Howe at Brooklyn Heights and later in New Jersey and Pennsylvania) they lost the opportunity to deal potentially mortal blows to the rebellion. There was also a grave lack of understanding and cooperation at crucial moments (as with Burgoyne and Howe in 1777). Finally, the British counted too strongly on loyalist support they did not receive.

But British mistakes alone could not account for the success of the United States. Feeble as their war effort occasionally became, the Americans were able generally to take advantage of their enemies' mistakes. The Continental Army, moreover, was by no means an inept force even before Steuben's reforms. The militias, while usually unreliable, could perform admirably under the leadership of men who understood them, like Arnold, Greene, and Morgan, and often reinforced the Continentals in crises. Furthermore, Washington, a rock in adversity, learned slowly but reasonably well the art of generalship. The supplies and funds furnished by France from 1776 to 1778 were invaluable, while French military and naval support after 1778 was essential. The outcome, therefore, resulted from a combination of British blunders, American efforts, and French assistance.

TREATY OF PARIS

The military verdict in North America was reflected in the preliminary Anglo-American peace treaty of 1782, which was included in the Treaty of Paris of 1783. Franklin, John Adams, John Jay, and Henry Laurens served as the American commissioners. By its terms Britain recognized the independence of the United States with generous boundaries, including the Mississippi River on the west. Britain retained Canada but ceded East and West Florida to Spain. Provisions were inserted calling for the payment of American private debts to British citizens, for American access to the Newfoundland fisheries, and for a recommendation by the

THE TREATY OF PARIS, MADE FINAL ON SEPTEMBER 3, 1783, ENDED THE AMERICAN REVOLUTION.

Continental Congress to the states in favor of fair treatment of the loyalists.

Most of the loyalists remained in the new country; however, perhaps as many as 80,000 Tories migrated to Canada, England, and the British West Indies. Many of these had served as British soldiers, and many had been banished by the American states. The loyalists were harshly treated as dangerous enemies by the American states during the war and immediately afterward. They were commonly deprived of civil rights, often fined, and frequently relieved of their property. The more conspicuous were usually banished upon pain of death. The British government compensated more than 4,000 of the exiles for property losses, paying out almost £3.3 million. It also gave them land grants, pensions, and appointments to enable them to reestablish themselves. The less ardent and more cautious Tories, staying in the United States, accepted the separation from Britain as final and, after the passage of a generation, could not be distinguished from the patriots.

FOUNDATIONS OF THE AMERICAN REPUBLIC

It had been far from certain that the Americans could fight a successful war against the might of Britain. The scattered colonies had little inherent unity; their experience of collective action was limited; an army had to be created and maintained; they had no common institutions other than the Continental Congress; and they had almost no experience of continental public finance. The Americans could not have hoped to win the war without French help, and the French monarchy—whose interests were anti-British but not pro-American—had waited watchfully to see what the Americans could do in the field. Although the French began supplying arms, clothing, and loans surreptitiously soon after the Americans declared independence, it was not until 1778 that a formal alliance was forged.

Most of these problems lasted beyond the achievement of independence and continued to vex American politics for many years, even for generations. Meanwhile, however, the colonies had valuable, though less visible, sources of strength. Practically all farmers had their own arms and could form into militia companies overnight. More fundamentally, Americans had for many years been receiving basically the same information, mainly from the English press, reprinted in identical form in colonial newspapers. The effect of this was to form a singularly wide body of agreed opinion about major public issues. Another force of incalculable importance was the fact that for several generations Americans had to a large extent been governing themselves through elected assemblies, which in turn had developed sophisticated experience in committee politics.

This factor of "institutional memory" was of great importance in the forming of a mentality of self-government. Men became attached to their habitual ways, especially when these were habitual ways of running their own affairs, and these habits formed the basis of an ideology just as pervasive and important to the people concerned as republican theories published in Britain and the European continent. Moreover, colonial self-government seemed, from a colonial point of view, to be continuous and consistent with the principles of English government—principles for which Parliament had fought the Civil Wars in the mid-17th century and which colonists believed to have been reestablished by the Glorious Revolution of 1688–89. It was equally important that experience of self-government had taught colonial leaders how to get things done. When the Continental Congress met in 1774, members did not have to debate procedure (except on voting); they already knew it. Finally, the Congress's authority was rooted in traditions of legitimacy. The old election laws were used. Voters could transfer their allegiance with minimal difficulty from the dying colonial assemblies to the new assemblies and conventions of the states.

PROBLEMS BEFORE THE SECOND CONTINENTAL CONGRESS

When the Second Continental Congress assembled in Philadelphia in May 1775, revolution was not a certainty. The Congress had to prepare for that contingency nevertheless and thus was confronted by two parallel sets of problems. The first was how to organize for war; the second, which proved less urgent but could not be set aside forever, was how to define the legal relationship between the Congress and the states.

In June 1775, in addition to appointing Washington (who had made a point of turning up in uniform) commander in chief, the Congress provided for the enlistment of an army. It then turned to the vexatious problems of finance. An aversion to taxation being one of the unities of American sentiment, the Congress began by trying to raise a domestic loan. It did not have much success, however, for the excellent reason that the outcome of the operation appeared highly dubious. At the same time, authority was taken for issuing a paper currency. This proved to be the most important method of domestic war finance, and, as the war years passed, Congress resorted to issuing more and more continental currency, which depreciated rapidly and had to compete with currencies issued by state governments. (People were inclined to prefer local currencies.) The Continental Army was a further source of a form of currency because its commission agents issued certificates in exchange for goods; these certificates bore an official promise of redemption and could be used in personal transactions. Loans raised overseas, notably in France and the Netherlands, were another important source of revenue.

In 1780 Congress decided to call in all former issues of currency and replace them with a new issue on a 40-to-1 ratio. The Philadelphia merchant Robert Morris, who was appointed superintendent of finance in 1781 and came to be known as "the Financier," guided the United States through its complex fiscal difficulties. Morris's personal finances were inextricably tangled up with those of the country, and he became the object of much hostile comment, but he also used his own resources to secure urgently

AS DEPICTED IN THIS CURRIER AND IVES PRINT, GEORGE WASHINGTON WAS APPOINTED AS COMMANDER IN CHIEF BY THE CONTINENTAL CONGRESS IN 1775.

needed loans from abroad. In 1781 Morris secured a charter for the first Bank of North America, an institution that owed much to the example of the Bank of England. Although the bank was attacked by radical egalitarians as an unrepublican manifestation of privilege, it gave the United States a firmer financial foundation.

The problem of financing and organizing the war sometimes overlapped with Congress's other major problem,

that of defining its relations with the states. The Congress, being only an association of states, had no power to tax individuals. The Articles of Confederation, a plan of government organization adopted and put into practice by Congress in 1777, although not officially ratified by all the states until 1781, gave Congress the right to make requisitions on the states proportionate to their ability to pay. The states in turn had to raise these sums by their own domestic powers to tax, a method that state legislators looking for reelection were reluctant to employ. The result was that many states were constantly in heavy arrears, and, particularly after the urgency of the war years had subsided, the Congress's ability to meet expenses and repay its war debts was crippled.

The Congress lacked power to enforce its requisitions and fell badly behind in repaying its wartime creditors. When individual states (Maryland as early as 1782, Pennsylvania in 1785) passed legislation providing for repayment of the debt owed to their own citizens by the Continental Congress, one of the reasons for the Congress's existence had begun to crumble. Two attempts were made to get the states to agree to grant the Congress the power it needed to raise revenue by levying an impost on imports. Each failed for want of unanimous consent. Essentially, an impost would have been collected at ports, which belonged to individual states—there was no "national" territory—and therefore cut across the concept of state sovereignty. Agreement was nearly obtained on each occasion, and, if it had been, the Constitutional Convention might never have been called. But the failure sharply pointed up the weakness of the Congress and of the union between the states under the Articles of Confederation.

The Articles of Confederation reflected strong preconceptions of state sovereignty. Article II expressly reserved sovereignty to the states individually, and another article even envisaged the possibility that one state might go to war without the others. Fundamental revisions could be made only with unanimous consent, because the Articles represented a treaty between sovereigns, not the creation of a new nation-state. Other major revisions required the consent of nine states. Yet state sovereignty principles rested on artificial foundations. The states could never have achieved independence on their own, and in fact the Congress had taken the first step both in recommending that the states form their own governments and in declaring their collective independence. Most important of its domestic responsibilities, by 1787 the Congress had enacted several ordinances establishing procedures for incorporating new territories. (It had been conflicts over western land claims that had held up ratification of the Articles. Eventually the states with western claims, principally New York and Virginia, ceded them to the United States.) The Northwest Ordinance of 1787 provided for the phased settlement and government of territories in the Ohio valley, leading to eventual admission as new states. It also excluded the introduction of slavery—though it did not exclude the retention of existing slaves.

The states had constantly looked to the Congress for leadership in the difficulties of war; now that the danger was past, however, disunity began to threaten to turn into disintegration.

ARTICLES OF CONFEDERATION

The Articles of Confederation were the first U.S. constitution (1781–89), which served as a bridge between the initial government by the Continental Congress of the Revolutionary period and the federal government provided under the U.S. Constitution of 1787. Because the experience of overbearing British central authority was vivid in colonial minds, the drafters of the Articles deliberately established a confederation of sovereign states. The Articles were written in 1776–77 and adopted by the Congress on Nov. 15, 1777. However, the document was not fully ratified by the states until March 1, 1781.

On paper, the Congress had power to regulate foreign affairs, war, and the postal service and to appoint military officers, control Indian affairs, borrow money, determine the value of coin, and issue bills of credit. In reality, however, the Articles gave the Congress no power to enforce its requests to the states for money or troops, and by the end of 1786 governmental effectiveness had broken down.

Nevertheless, some solid accomplishments had been achieved: certain state claims to western lands were settled, and the Northwest Ordinance of 1787 established the fundamental pattern of evolving government in the territories north of the Ohio River. Equally important, the Articles of Confederation provided the new nation with instructive experience in self-government under a written document. In revealing their own weaknesses, the Articles paved the way for the Constitutional Convention of 1787 and the present form of U.S. government.

The Congress was largely discredited in the eyes of a wide range of influential men, representing both old and new interests. The states were setting up their own tariff barriers against each other and quarreling among themselves; virtual war had broken out between competing settlers from Pennsylvania and Connecticut claiming the same lands. By 1786, well-informed men were discussing a probable breakup of the confederation into three or more new groups, which could have led to wars between the American republics.

NORTHWEST ORDINANCES

The Northwest Ordinances, also called Ordinances of 1784, 1785, and 1787, were several ordinances enacted by the U.S. Congress for the purpose of establishing orderly and equitable procedures for the settlement and political incorporation of the Northwest Territory (i.e., that part of the American frontier lying west of Pennsylvania, north of the Ohio River, east of the Mississippi River, and south of the Great Lakes; this is the area known today as the American Midwest).

Until about 1780 the lands of the Northwest Territory were claimed by several existing states, including New York and Virginia. These states soon ceded their territorial holdings to the central government, and by the time that the American Revolution ended in 1783, specific measures were needed to guide the settlement and division of the Northwest Territory. The Ordinance of 1784, drafted by Thomas Jefferson and passed by Congress, divided the territory into a handful of self-governing districts. It stipulated that each district could send one representative to Congress upon its attaining a population of 20,000, and it would become eligible for statehood when its population equaled that of the least populous existing state. (This ordinance was superseded by the Ordinance of 1787.)

The Ordinance of 1785 provided for the scientific surveying of the territory's lands and for a systematic subdivision of them. Land was to be subdivided according to a rectangular grid system; the basic unit of land grant was the township, which was a square area measuring six miles on each side. A township could then be subdivided into a number of rectangular parcels of individually owned land. The minimum land sale was set at one square mile (640 acres), and the minimum price per acre was one dollar. One section in each township was to be set aside for a school. These procedures formed the basis of American public land policy until the Homestead Act of 1862.

The Northwest Ordinance of 1787, the most important of the three acts, laid the basis for the government of the Northwest Territory and for the admission of its constituent parts as states into the Union. Under this ordinance, each district was to be governed by a governor and judges appointed by Congress until it attained a population of 5,000 adult free males, at which time it would become a territory and could form its own representative legislature. The Northwest Territory must eventually comprise a minimum of three and a maximum of five states; an individual territory could be admitted to statehood in the Union after having attained a population of 60,000. Under the ordinance, slavery was forever outlawed from the lands of the Northwest Territory; freedom of religion and other civil liberties were guaranteed; the resident Indians were promised decent treatment; and education was provided for. Under this ordinance, the principle of granting new states equal rather than inferior status to older ones was firmly established. The ordinances were a major accomplishment of the often-maligned government under the Articles of Confederation.

THOMAS JEFFERSON (SHOWN HERE ON THE LEFT, WITH BENJAMIN FRANKLIN) DRAFTED THE ORIGINAL ORDINANCE OF 1784, WHICH DIVIDED THE TERRITORY INTO DISTRICTS THAT WOULD GOVERN THEMSELVES.

STATE POLITICS

The problems of forming a new government affected the states individually as well as in confederation. Most of them established their own constitutions—formulated either in conventions or in the existing assemblies. The most democratic of these constitutions was the product of a virtual revolution in Pennsylvania, where a highly organized radical party seized the opportunity of the revolutionary crisis to gain power. Suffrage was put on a taxpayer basis, with nearly all adult males paying some tax; representation was reformed to bring in the populations of western counties; and a single-chamber legislature was established. An oath of loyalty to the constitution for some time excluded political opponents and particularly Quakers (who could not take oaths) from participation. The constitutions of the other states reflected the firm political ascendancy of the traditional ruling elite. Power ascended from a broad base in the elective franchise and representation through a narrowing hierarchy of offices restricted by property qualifications. State governors had in some cases to be men of great wealth. Senators were either wealthy or elected by the wealthy sector of the electorate. (These conditions were not invariable; Virginia, which had a powerful landed elite, dispensed with such restrictions.) Several states retained religious qualifications for office; the separation of church and state was not a popular concept, and minorities such as Baptists and Quakers were subjected to indignities that amounted in some places (notably Massachusetts and Connecticut) to forms of persecution.

Elite power provided a lever for one of the most significant transformations of the era, one that took place almost without being either noticed or intended. This was the acceptance of the principle of giving representation in legislative bodies in proportion to population. It was made not only possible but attractive when the larger aggregations of population broadly coincided with the highest concentrations of property: Great merchants and landowners from populous areas could continue to exert political ascendancy so long as they retained some sort of hold on the political process. The principle reemerged to dominate the distribution of voters in the House of Representatives and in the electoral college under the new federal Constitution.

Relatively conservative constitutions did little to stem a tide of increasingly democratic politics. The old elites had to wrestle with new political forces (and in the process they learned how to organize in the new regime). Executive power was weakened. Many elections were held annually, and terms were limited. Legislatures quickly admitted new representatives from recent settlements, many with little previous political experience.

The new state governments, moreover, had to tackle major issues that affected all classes. The needs of public finance led to emissions of paper money. In several states these were resumed after the war, and, since they tended (though not invariably) to depreciate, they led directly to fierce controversies. The treatment of loyalists was also a theme of intense political dispute after the war. Despite the protests of men such as Alexander Hamilton, who urged restoration of property and rights, in many states loyalists were driven out and their estates seized and redistributed in forms of auction, providing opportunities for speculation rather than personal occupation. Many states were depressed economically. In Massachusetts, which remained under orthodox control, stiff taxation under conditions of postwar depression trapped many farmers into debt. Unable to meet their obligations, they rose late in 1786 under a Revolutionary War officer, Capt. Daniel Shays, in a movement to prevent the court sessions. Shays's Rebellion was crushed early in 1787 by an army raised in the state. The action caused only a few casualties, but the episode sent a shiver of fear throughout the country's propertied classes. It also seemed to justify the classical thesis that republics were unstable. It thus provided a potent stimulus to state legislatures to send delegates to the convention called (following a preliminary meeting in

Annapolis) to meet at Philadelphia to revise the Articles of Confederation.

THE CONSTITUTIONAL CONVENTION

The Philadelphia Convention, which met in May 1787, was officially called for by the old Congress solely to remedy defects in the Articles of Confederation. But the Virginia Plan presented by the Virginia delegates went beyond revision and boldly proposed to introduce a new, national government in place of the existing confederation. The convention thus immediately faced the question of whether the United States was to be a country in the modern sense or would continue as a weak federation of autonomous and equal states represented in a single chamber, which was the principle embodied in the New Jersey Plan presented by several small states. This decision was effectively made when a compromise plan for a bicameral legislature—one house with representation based on population and one with equal representation for all states—was approved in mid-July. Though neither plan prevailed, the new national government in its final form was endowed with broad powers that made it indisputably national and superior.

The Constitution, as it emerged after a summer of debate, embodied a much stronger principle of separation of powers than was generally to be found in the state constitutions. The chief executive was to be a single figure (a composite executive was discussed and rejected) and was to be elected by an electoral college, meeting in the states. This followed much debate over the

Virginia Plan's preference for legislative election. The principal control on the chief executive, or president, against violation of the Constitution was the rather remote threat of impeachment (to which James Madison attached great importance). The Virginia Plan's proposal that representation be proportional to population in both houses was severely modified by the retention of equal representation for each state in the Senate. But the question of whether to count slaves in the population was abrasive. After some contention, antislavery forces gave way to a compromise by which three-fifths of the slaves would be counted as population for purposes of representation (and direct taxation). Slave states would thus be perpetually overrepresented in national politics; provision was also added for a law permitting the recapture of fugitive slaves, though in deference to republican scruples the word "slaves" was not used.

Contemporary theory expected the legislature to be the most powerful branch of government. Thus, to balance the system, the executive was given a veto, and a judicial system with powers of review was established. It was also implicit in the structure that the new federal judiciary would have power to veto any state laws that conflicted either with the Constitution or with federal statutes. States were forbidden to pass laws impairing obligations of contract—a measure aimed at encouraging capital—and the Congress could pass no ex post facto law. But the Congress was endowed with the basic powers of a modern—and sovereign—government. This was a republic, and the United States could confer no aristocratic titles of honour. The prospect of eventual enlargement of federal power appeared in the clause giving the Congress powers to pass legislation "necessary and proper" for implementing the general purposes of the Constitution.

THE FOUNDING FATHERS AND SLAVERY

Although many of the Founding Fathers acknowledged that slavery violated the core American Revolutionary ideal of liberty, their simultaneous commitment to private property rights, principles of limited government, and intersectional harmony prevented them from making a bold move against slavery. The considerable investment of southern Founders in slave-based staple agriculture, combined with their deep-seated racial prejudice, posed additional obstacles to emancipation.

In his initial draft of the Declaration of Independence, Thomas Jefferson condemned the injustice of the slave trade and, by implication, slavery, but he also blamed the presence of enslaved Africans in North America on avaricious British colonial policies. Jefferson thus acknowledged that slavery violated the natural rights of the enslaved, while at the same time he absolved Americans of any responsibility for owning slaves themselves. The Continental Congress apparently rejected the tortured logic of this passage by deleting it from the final document, but this decision also signaled the Founders' commitment to subordinating the controversial issue of slavery to the larger goal of securing the unity and independence of the United States.

Nevertheless, the Founders, with the exception of those from South Carolina and Georgia, exhibited considerable aversion to slavery during the era of the Articles of Confederation (1781–89) by prohibiting the importation of foreign slaves to individual states and lending their support to a proposal by Jefferson to ban slavery in the Northwest Territory. Such antislavery policies, however, only went so far. The prohibition of foreign slave imports, by limiting the foreign supply, conveniently served the interests of Virginia and Maryland

(continued on the next page)

61

THE FOUNDING FATHERS AND SLAVERY (CONTINUED)

slaveholders, who could then sell their own surplus slaves southward and westward at higher prices. Furthermore, the ban on slavery in the Northwest tacitly legitimated the expansion of slavery in the Southwest.

Despite initial disagreements over slavery at the Constitutional Convention in 1787, the Founders once again demonstrated their commitment to maintaining the unity of the new United States by resolving to diffuse sectional tensions over slavery. To this end the Founders drafted a series of constitutional clauses acknowledging deep-seated regional differences over slavery while requiring all sections of the new country to make compromises as well. They granted slaveholding states the right to count three-fifths of their slave population when it came to apportioning the number of a state's representatives to Congress, thereby enhancing southern power in the House of Representatives. But they also used this same ratio to determine the federal tax contribution required of each state, thus increasing the direct federal tax burden of slaveholding states. Georgians and South Carolinians won a moratorium until 1808 on any congressional ban against the importation of slaves, but in the meantime individual states remained free to prohibit slave imports if they so wished. Southerners also obtained the inclusion of a fugitive slave clause designed to encourage the return of runaway slaves who sought refuge in free states, but the Constitution left enforcement of this clause to the cooperation of the states rather than to the coercion of Congress.

Although the Founders, consistent with their beliefs in limited government, opposed granting the new federal government significant authority over slavery, several individual northern Founders promoted antislavery causes at the state level. Benjamin Franklin in Pennsylvania, as well as John Jay and Alexander Hamilton in New York, served as officers in their respective state antislavery societies. The prestige they lent to these organizations ultimately contributed to the gradual abolition of slavery in each of the northern states.

Although slavery was legal in every northern state at the beginning of the American Revolution, its economic impact was marginal. As a result, northern Founders were freer to explore the libertarian dimensions of Revolutionary ideology. The experience of Franklin was in many ways typical of the evolving attitudes of northern Founders toward slavery. Although enmeshed in the slave system for much of his life, Franklin eventually came to believe that slavery ought to be abolished gradually and legally. Franklin himself had owned slaves, run ads in his *Pennsylvania Gazette* to secure the return of fugitive slaves, and defended the honor of slaveholding revolutionaries. By 1781, however, Franklin had divested himself of slaves, and shortly thereafter he became the president of the Pennsylvania Abolition Society. He also went further than most of his contemporaries by signing a petition to the First Federal Congress in 1790 for the abolition of slavery and the slave trade.

Unlike their northern counterparts, southern Founders generally steered clear of organized antislavery activities, primarily to maintain their legitimacy among slaveholding constituents. Furthermore, while a few northern and southern Founders manumitted a small number of slaves, no southern plantation-owning Founder, except George Washington, freed a sizeable body of enslaved laborers. Because his own slaves shared familial attachments with the dower slaves of his wife, Martha Custis Washington, he sought to convince her heirs to forego their inheritance rights in favor of a collective manumission so as to ensure that entire families, not just individual family members, might be freed. Washington failed to win the consent of the Custis heirs, but he nevertheless made sure, through his last will and testament, that his own slaves would enjoy the benefit of freedom.

(*continued on the next page*)

63

THE FOUNDING FATHERS AND SLAVERY (CONTINUED)

Washington's act of manumission implied that he could envision a biracial United States where both blacks and whites might live together as free people. Jefferson, however, explicitly rejected this vision. He acknowledged that slavery violated the natural rights of slaves and that conflicts over slavery might one day lead to the dissolution of the union, but he also believed that, given alleged innate racial differences and deeply held prejudices, emancipation would inevitably degrade the character of the republic and unleash violent civil strife between blacks and whites. Jefferson thus advocated coupling emancipation with what he called "colonization," or removal, of the black population beyond the boundaries of the United States. His proposals won considerable support in the North, where racial prejudice was on the rise, but such schemes found little support among the majority of southern slaveholders.

When the last remaining Founders died in the 1830s, they left behind an ambiguous legacy with regard to slavery. They had succeeded in gradually abolishing slavery in the northern states and northwestern territories but permitted its rapid expansion in the South and Southwest. Although they eventually enacted a federal ban on the importation of foreign slaves in 1808, the enslaved population continued to expand through natural reproduction, while the growing internal domestic slave trade led to an increase in the tragic breakup of enslaved families.

The states retained their civil jurisdiction, but there was an emphatic shift of the political centre of gravity to the federal government, of which the most fundamental indication was the universal understanding that this government would act directly on citizens, as individuals, throughout all the states, regardless of state authority. The language of the Constitution told of the new style: It began, "We the people of the United States," rather than "We the people of New Hampshire, Massachusetts, etc."

The draft Constitution aroused widespread opposition. Anti-Federalists—so-called because their opponents deftly seized the appellation of "Federalists," though they were really nationalists—were strong in states such as Virginia, New York, and Massachusetts, where the economy was relatively successful and many people saw little need for such extreme remedies. Anti-Federalists also expressed fears—here touches of class conflict certainly arose—that the new government would fall into the hands of merchants and men of money. Many good republicans detected oligarchy in the structure of the Senate, with its six-year terms. The absence of a bill of rights aroused deep fears of central power. The Federalists, however, had the advantages of communications, the press, organization, and, generally, the better of the argument. Anti-Federalists also suffered the disadvantage of having no internal coherence or unified purpose.

The debate gave rise to a very intensive literature, much of it at a very high level. The most sustained pro-Federalist argument, written mainly by Hamilton and Madison (assisted by Jay) under the pseudonym Publius, appeared in the newspapers as *The Federalist*. These essays attacked the feebleness of the confederation and claimed that the new Constitution would have advantages for all sectors of society while threatening none. In the course of the debate, they passed from a strongly nationalist standpoint to one that showed more respect for the idea of a mixed form of government that would safeguard the states. Madison contributed assurances that a multiplicity of interests would counteract each other, preventing the consolidation of power continually charged by their enemies.

The Bill of Rights, steered through the first Congress by Madison's diplomacy, mollified much of the latent opposition. These first 10 amendments, ratified in 1791, adopted into the Constitution the basic English common-law rights that Americans had fought for. But they did more. Unlike Britain, the United States secured a guarantee of freedom for the press and the right of (peaceable) assembly. Also unlike Britain, church and state were formally separated in a clause that seemed to set equal value on nonestablishment of religion and its free exercise. (This left the states free to maintain their own establishments.)

In state conventions held through the winter of 1787 to the summer of 1788, the Constitution was ratified by the necessary minimum of nine states. But the vote was desperately close in Virginia and New York, respectively the 10th and 11th states to ratify, and without them the whole scheme would have been built on sand.

THE SOCIAL REVOLUTION AND THE NEW REPUBLIC

The American Revolution was a great social upheaval but one that was widely diffused, often gradual, and different in different regions. The principles of liberty and equality stood in stark conflict with the institution of African slavery, which had built much of the country's wealth. One gradual effect of this conflict was the decline of slavery in all the northern states; another was a spate of manumissions by liberal slave owners in Virginia. But with most slave owners, especially in South Carolina and Georgia, ideals counted for nothing. Throughout the slave states, the institution of slavery came to be reinforced by a white supremacist doctrine of racial inferiority. The manumissions did result in the development of new communities of free blacks, who enjoyed considerable freedom of movement for a few years and who produced some outstanding figures, such as the astronomer Benjamin Banneker and the religious leader Richard Allen, a founder of the African Methodist Episcopal Church Zion. But in the 1790s and after, the condition of free blacks deteriorated as states adopted laws restricting their activities, residences, and economic choices. In general they came to occupy poor neighbourhoods and grew into a permanent underclass, denied education and opportunity.

The American Revolution also dramatized the economic importance of women. Women had always contributed indispensably to the operation of farms and often businesses, while they seldom acquired independent status; but, when war removed men from the locality, women often had to take full charge, which they proved they could do. Republican ideas spread among women, influencing discussion of women's rights, education, and role in society. Some states modified their inheritance and property laws to permit women to inherit a share of estates and to exercise limited control of property after marriage. On the whole, however, the Revolution itself had only very gradual and diffused effects on women's ultimate status. Such changes as took place amounted to a fuller recognition of the importance of women as mothers of republican citizens rather than making them into independent citizens of equal political and civil status with men.

Americans had fought for independence to protect common-law rights; they had no program for legal reform. Gradually, however, some customary practices came to seem out of keeping with republican principles. The outstanding example was the law of inheritance. The new states took steps, where necessary, to remove the old rule of primogeniture in favour of equal partition of intestate estates; this conformed to

DURING THE AMERICAN REVOLUTION, WOMEN ROSE TO THE OCCASION AND PROVED THAT THEY WERE JUST AS CAPABLE AS MEN WHEN IT CAME TO OPERATING BUSINESSES AND FARMS.

both the egalitarian and the individualist principles preferred by American society. Humanization of the penal codes, however, occurred only gradually, in the 19th century, inspired as much by European example as by American sentiment.

RELIGIOUS REVIVALISM

Religion played a central role in the emergence of a distinctively "American" society in the first years of independence. Several key developments took place. One was the creation of American denominations independent of their British and European origins and leadership. By 1789, American Anglicans (renaming themselves Episcopalians), Methodists (formerly Wesleyans), Roman Catholics, and members of various Baptist, Lutheran, and Dutch Reformed congregations had established organizations and chosen leaders who were born in or full-time residents of what had become the United States of America. Another pivotal postindependence development was a rekindling of religious enthusiasm, especially on the frontier, that opened the gates of religious activism to the laity. Still another was the disestablishment of tax-supported churches in those states most deeply feeling the impact of democratic diversity. And finally, this period saw the birth of a liberal and socially aware version of Christianity uniting Enlightenment values with American activism.

Between 1798 and 1800 a sudden burst of revitalization shook frontier Protestant congregations, beginning with a great revival in Logan county, Ky., under the leadership of men such as James McGready and the brothers John and William McGee. This was followed by a gigantic camp meeting at Cane Ridge, where thousands were "converted." The essence of the frontier revival was that this conversion from mere formal Christianity to a full conviction in God's mercy for the sinner was a deeply emotional experience accessible even to those with much faith and little learning. So exhorters who were barely literate themselves could preach brimstone and fire and showers of grace, bringing repentant listeners to a state of excitement in which they would weep and groan, writhe and faint, and undergo physical transports in full public view.

"Heart religion" supplanted "head religion." For the largely Scotch-Irish Presbyterian ministers in the West, this led to dangerous territory because the official church leadership preferred more decorum and biblical scholarship from its pastors. Moreover, the idea of winning salvation by noisy penitence undercut Calvinist predestination. In fact, the fracture along fault lines of class and geography led to several schisms. Methodism had fewer problems of this kind. It never embraced predestination, and, more to the point, its structure was democratic, with rudimentarily educated lay preachers able to rise from leading individual congregations to presiding over districts and regional "conferences," eventually embracing the entire church membership. Methodism fitted very neatly into frontier conditions through its use of traveling ministers, or circuit riders, who rode from isolated settlement to settlement, saving souls and mightily liberalizing the word of God.

The revival spirit rolled back eastward to inspire a "Second Great Awakening," especially in New England, that emphasized gatherings that were less uninhibited than camp meetings but warmer than conventional Congregational and Presbyterian services. Ordained and college-educated ministers such as Lyman Beecher made it their mission to promote revivalism as a counterweight to the Deism of some of the Founding Fathers and the atheism of the French Revolution. Revivals also gave churches a new grasp on the loyalties of their congregations through lay participation in spreading the good word of salvation. This voluntarism more than offset the gradual state-by-state cancellation of taxpayer support for individual denominations.

The era of the early republic also saw the growth, especially among the urban educated elite of Boston, of a gentler form of Christianity embodied in Unitarianism, which

THIS PRINT SHOWS AN EARLY 19TH-CENTURY METHODIST CAMP MEETING.

rested on the notion of an essentially benevolent God who made his will known to humankind through their exercise of the reasoning powers bestowed on them. In the Unitarian view, Jesus Christ was simply a great moral teacher. Many Christians of the "middling" sort viewed Unitarianism as excessively concerned with ideas and social reform and far too indulgent or indifferent to the existence of sin and Satan. By 1815, then, the social structure of American Protestantism, firmly embedded in many activist forms in the national culture, had taken shape.

THE FEDERALIST ADMINISTRATION AND THE FORMATION OF PARTIES

The first elections under the new Constitution were held in 1789. George Washington was unanimously voted the country's first president. His secretary of the treasury, Alexander Hamilton, formed a clear-cut program that soon gave substance to the old fears of the Anti-Federalists. Hamilton, who had believed since the early 1780s that a national debt would be "a national blessing," both for economic reasons and because it would act as a "cement" to the union, used his new power base to realize the ambitions of the nationalists. He recommended that the federal government pay off the old Continental Congress's debts at par rather than at a depreciated value and that it assume state debts, drawing the interests of the creditors toward the central government rather than state governments. This plan met strong opposition from the many who had sold their securities at great discount during the postwar depression and from southern states, which had

THE FOUNDING FATHERS, DEISM, AND CHRISTIANITY

For some time the question of the religious faith of the Founding Fathers has generated a culture war in the United States. Scholars trained in research universities have generally argued that the majority of the Founders were religious rationalists or Unitarians. Pastors and other writers who identify themselves as Evangelicals have claimed not only that most of the Founders held orthodox beliefs but also that some were born-again Christians.

Whatever their beliefs, the Founders came from similar religious backgrounds. Most were Protestants. The largest number were raised in the three largest Christian traditions of colonial America—Anglicanism (as in the cases of John Jay, George Washington, and Edward Rutledge), Presbyterianism (as in the cases of Richard Stockton and the Rev. John Witherspoon), and Congregationalism (as in the cases of John Adams and Samuel Adams). Other Protestant groups included the Society of Friends (Quakers), the Lutherans, and the Dutch Reformed. Three Founders—Charles Carroll and Daniel Carroll of Maryland and Thomas Fitzsimmons of Pennsylvania—were of Roman Catholic heritage.

The sweeping disagreement over the religious faiths of the Founders arises from a question of discrepancy. Did their private beliefs differ from the orthodox teachings of their churches? On the surface, most Founders appear to have been orthodox (or "right-believing") Christians. Most were baptized, listed on church rolls, married to practicing Christians, and frequent or at least sporadic attenders of services of Christian worship. In public statements, most invoked divine assistance.

But the widespread existence in 18th-century America of a school of religious thought called Deism complicates the actual beliefs of the

Founders. Drawing from the scientific and philosophical work of such figures as Jean-Jacques Rousseau, Isaac Newton, and John Locke, Deists argued that human experience and rationality—rather than religious dogma and mystery—determine the validity of human beliefs. In his widely read *The Age of Reason*, Thomas Paine, the principal American exponent of Deism, called Christianity "a fable." Paine, the protégé of Benjamin Franklin, denied "that the Almighty ever did communicate anything to man, by . . . speech . . . language, or . . . vision." Postulating a distant deity whom he called "Nature's God" (a term also used in the Declaration of Independence), Paine declared in a "profession of faith":

I believe in one God, and no more; and I hope for happiness beyond this life. I believe in the equality of man; and I believe that religious duties consist in doing justice, loving mercy, and in endeavoring to make our fellow-creatures happy.

Thus, Deism inevitably subverted orthodox Christianity. Persons influenced by the movement had little reason to read the Bible, to pray, to attend church, or to participate in such rites as baptism, Holy Communion, and the laying on of hands (confirmation) by bishops. With the notable exceptions of Abigail Adams and Dolley Madison, Deism seems to have had little effect on women. For example, Martha Washington, the daughters of Thomas Jefferson, and Elizabeth Kortright Monroe and her daughters seem to have held orthodox Christian beliefs.

But Deistic thought was immensely popular in colleges from the middle of the 18th into the 19th century. Thus, it influenced many educated (as well as uneducated) males of the Revolutionary generation. Although such men would generally continue their public affiliation with Christianity after college, they might inwardly hold unorthodox religious views. Depending on the extent to which Americans of Christian background were influenced by Deism, their religious beliefs would fall into three categories: non-Christian

(*continued on the next page*)

THE FOUNDING FATHERS, DEISM, AND CHRISTIANITY (CONTINUED)

Deism, Christian Deism, and orthodox Christianity.

One can differentiate a Founding Father influenced by Deism from an orthodox Christian believer by following certain criteria. Anyone seeking the answer should consider at least the following four points. First, an inquirer should examine the Founder's church involvement. However, because a colonial church served not only religious but also social and political functions, church attendance or service in a governing body (such as an Anglican vestry, which was a state office in colonies such as Maryland, Virginia, and South Carolina) fails to guarantee a Founder's orthodoxy. But Founders who were believing Christians would nevertheless be more likely to go to church than those influenced by Deism.

The second consideration is an evaluation of the participation of a Founder in the ordinances or sacraments of his church. Most had no choice about being baptized as children, but as adults they did have a choice about participating in communion or (if Episcopalian or Roman Catholic) in confirmation. And few Founders who were Deists would have participated in either rite. George Washington's refusal to receive communion in his adult life indicated Deistic belief to many of his pastors and peers.

Third, one should note the religious language a Founder used. Non-Christian Deists such as Paine refused to use Judeo-Christian terminology and described God with such expressions as "Providence," "the Creator," "the Ruler of Great Events," and "Nature's God." Founders who fall into the category of Christian Deists used Deistic terms for God but sometimes added a Christian dimension—such as "Merciful Providence" or "Divine Goodness." Yet these Founders did not move further into orthodoxy and employ the traditional language of Christian piety. Founders who remained unaffected by Deism or who (like John Adams) became conservative Unitarians used terms that clearly conveyed their orthodoxy ("Savior," "Redeemer," "Resurrected Christ").

Finally, one should consider what friends, family, and, above all, clergy said about a Founder's religious faith. That Washington's pastors in Philadelphia clearly viewed him as significantly influenced by Deism says more about Washington's faith than do the opposite views of later writers or the cloudy memories of a few Revolutionary veterans who avowed Washington's orthodoxy decades after his death.

Although no examination of history can capture the inner faith of any person, these four indicators can help locate the Founders on the religious spectrum. Ethan Allen, for example, appears clearly to have been a non-Christian Deist. James Monroe, a close friend of Paine, remained officially an Episcopalian but may have stood closer to non-Christian Deism than to Christian Deism. Founders who fall into the category of Christian Deists include Washington (whose dedication to Christianity was clear in his own mind), John Adams, and, with some qualifications, Thomas Jefferson. Jefferson was more influenced by the reason-centred Enlightenment than either Adams or Washington. Orthodox Christians among the Founders include the staunchly Calvinistic Samuel Adams. John Jay (who served as president of the American Bible Society), Elias Boudinot (who wrote a book on the imminent Second Coming of Jesus), and Patrick Henry (who distributed religious tracts while riding circuit as a lawyer) clearly believed in Evangelical Christianity.

Although orthodox Christians participated at every stage of the new republic, Deism influenced a majority of the Founders. The movement opposed barriers to moral improvement and to social justice. It stood for rational inquiry, for skepticism about dogma and mystery, and for religious toleration. Many of its adherents advocated universal education, freedom of the press, and separation

(continued on the next page)

THE FOUNDING FATHERS, DEISM, AND CHRISTIANITY (CONTINUED)

THIS 19TH-CENTURY ILLUSTRATION SHOWS A SWORD-WIELDING ETHAN ALLEN CAPTURING FORT TICONDEROGA, NEW YORK, IN 1775. ALLEN WAS KNOWN TO BE A NON-CHRISTIAN DEIST.

of church and state. If the nation owes much to the Judeo-Christian tradition, it is also indebted to Deism, a movement of reason and equality that influenced the Founding Fathers to embrace liberal political ideals remarkable for their time.

repudiated their debts and did not want to be taxed to pay other states' debts. A compromise in Congress was reached—thanks to the efforts of Secretary of State Jefferson—whereby southern states approved Hamilton's plan in return for northern agreement to fix the location of the new national capital on the banks of the Potomac, closer to the South. When Hamilton next introduced his plan to found a Bank of the United States, modeled on the Bank of England, opposition began to harden. Many argued that the Constitution did not confide this power to Congress. Hamilton, however, persuaded Washington that anything not expressly forbidden by the Constitution was permitted under implied powers—the beginning of "loose" as opposed to "strict" constructionist interpretations of the Constitution. The Bank Act passed in 1791. Hamilton also advocated plans for the support of nascent industry, which proved premature, and he imposed the revenue-raising whiskey excise that led to the Whiskey Rebellion, a minor uprising in western Pennsylvania in 1794.

A party opposed to Hamilton's fiscal policies began to form in Congress. With Madison at its centre and with support from Jefferson, it soon extended its appeal beyond Congress to popular constituencies. Meanwhile, the French Revolution and France's subsequent declaration of war against Great Britain, Spain, and Holland further divided American loyalties. Democratic-Republican societies sprang up to express support for France, while Hamilton and his supporters, known as Federalists, backed Britain for economic reasons. Washington pronounced American neutrality in Europe, but to prevent a war with Britain he sent Chief Justice John Jay to London to negotiate a treaty. In the Jay Treaty (1794) the United States gained only minor concessions and—humiliatingly—accepted British naval supremacy as the price of protection for American shipping.

Washington, whose tolerance had been severely strained by the Whiskey Rebellion and by criticism of the Jay Treaty, chose not to run for a third presidential term. In his Farewell Address, in a passage drafted by Hamilton, he denounced the new party politics as divisive and dangerous. Parties did not yet aspire to national objectives, however, and, when the Federalist John Adams was elected president, the Democrat-Republican Jefferson, as the presidential candidate with the second greatest number of votes, became vice president. Wars in Europe and on the high seas, together with rampant opposition at home, gave the new administration little peace. Virtual naval war with France had followed from American acceptance of British naval protection. In 1798 a French attempt to solicit bribes from American commissioners negotiating a settlement of differences (the so-called XYZ Affair) aroused a wave of anti-French feeling. Later that year the Federalist majority in Congress passed the Alien and Sedition Acts, which imposed serious civil restrictions on aliens suspected of pro-French activities and penalized U.S. citizens who criticized the government, making nonsense of the First Amendment's guarantee of free press. The acts were most often invoked to prosecute Republican editors, some of whom served jail terms. These measures in turn called forth the Virginia and Kentucky resolutions, drafted respectively by Madison and Jefferson, which invoked state sovereignty against intolerable federal powers. War with France often seemed imminent during this period, but Adams was determined to avoid issuing a formal declaration of war, and in this he succeeded.

Taxation, which had been levied to pay anticipated war costs, brought more discontent, however, including a new minor rising in Pennsylvania led by Jacob Fries. Fries's Rebellion was

TRIUMPHAL ARCHES, SUCH AS THIS ONE NEAR PHILADELPHIA, WERE ERECTED THROUGHOUT THE UNITED STATES TO COMMEMORATE THE INAUGURATION OF PRES. GEORGE WASHINGTON ON APRIL 30, 1789.

put down without difficulty, but widespread disagreement over issues ranging from civil liberties to taxation was polarizing American politics. A basic sense of political identity now divided Federalists from Republicans, and in the election of 1800 Jefferson drew on deep sources of Anti-Federalist opposition to challenge and defeat his old friend and colleague Adams. The result was the first contest over the presidency between political parties and the first actual change of government as a result of a general election in modern history.

JEFFERSON REPUBLICANS IN POWER

Jefferson began his presidency with a plea for reconciliation: "We are all Republicans, we are all Federalists." He had no plans for a permanent two-party system of government. He also began with a strong commitment to limited government and strict construction of the Constitution. All these commitments were soon to be tested by the exigencies of war, diplomacy, and political contingency.

On the American continent, Jefferson pursued a policy of expansion. He seized the opportunity when Napoleon I decided to relinquish French ambitions in North America by offering the Louisiana territory for sale (Spain had recently ceded the territory to France). This extraordinary acquisition, the Louisiana Purchase, bought at a price of a few cents per acre, more than doubled the area of the United States. Jefferson had no constitutional sanction for such an exercise of executive power; he made up the rules as he went along, taking a broad construction view of the Constitution on this issue. He also sought opportunities to gain Florida from Spain, and, for scientific and political reasons, he sent Meriwether Lewis and William Clark on an expedition of exploration across the continent. This territorial expansion was not without problems. Various separatist movements periodically arose, including a plan for a Northern Confederacy formulated by New England Federalists. Aaron Burr, who had been elected Jefferson's vice president in 1800 but was replaced in 1804, led several western conspiracies. Arrested and tried for treason, he was acquitted in 1807.

JAMES MADISON, WHO WAS INTEGRAL TO THE PLANNING AND RATIFICATION OF THE U.S. CONSTITUTION AND CONTRIBUTED TO THE FEDERALIST PAPERS, BECAME THE FOURTH PRESIDENT OF THE UNITED STATES IN 1809.

As chief executive, Jefferson clashed with members of the judiciary, many of whom had been late appointments by Adams. One of his primary opponents was the late appointee Chief Justice John Marshall, most notably in the case of *Marbury v. Madison* (1803), in which the Supreme Court first exercised the power of judicial review of congressional legislation.

By the start of Jefferson's second term in office, Europe was engulfed in the Napoleonic Wars. The United States remained neutral, but both Britain and France imposed various orders and decrees severely restricting American trade with Europe and confiscated American ships for violating the new rules. Britain also conducted impressment raids in which U.S. citizens were sometimes seized. Unable to agree to treaty terms with Britain, Jefferson tried to coerce both Britain and France into ceasing to violate "neutral rights" with a total embargo on American exports, enacted by Congress in 1807. The results were catastrophic for American commerce and produced bitter alienation in New England, where the embargo (written backward as "O grab me") was held to be a southern plot to destroy New England's wealth. In 1809, shortly after Madison was elected president, the embargo act was repealed.

SECOND WAR OF AMERICAN INDEPENDENCE

Madison's presidency was dominated by foreign affairs. Both Britain and France committed depredations on American shipping, but Britain was more resented, partly because with the greatest navy it was more effective and partly because

ANDREW JACKSON DURING THE BATTLE OF NEW ORLEANS, ILLUSTRATION BY FREDERICK COFFAY YOHN, C. 1922.

Americans were extremely sensitive to British insults to national honour. Certain expansionist elements looking to both Florida and Canada began to press for war and took advantage of the issue of naval protection. Madison's own aim was to preserve the principle of freedom of the seas and to assert the ability of the United States to protect its own interests and its citizens. While striving to confront the European adversaries impartially, he was drawn into war against Britain, which was declared in June 1812 on a vote of 79–49 in the House and 19–13 in the Senate. There was almost no support for war in the strong Federalist New England states.

The War of 1812 began and ended in irony. The British had already rescinded the offending orders in council, but the news had not reached the United States at the time of the declaration. The Americans were poorly placed from every point of view. Ideological objections to armies and navies had been responsible for a minimal naval force. Ideological objections to banks had been responsible, in 1812, for the Senate's refusal to renew the charter of the Bank of the United States. Mercantile sentiment was hostile to the administration. Under the circumstances, it was remarkable that the United States succeeded in staggering through two years of war, eventually winning important naval successes at sea, on the Great Lakes, and on Lake Champlain. On land a British raiding party burned public buildings in Washington, D.C., and drove President Madison to flee from the capital. The only action with long-term implications was Andrew Jackson's victory at the Battle of New Orleans—won in January 1815, two weeks after peace had been achieved with the signing of the Treaty of Ghent (Belg.). Jackson's political reputation rose directly from this battle.

In historical retrospect, the most important aspect of the peace settlement was an agreement to set up a boundary commission for the Canadian border, which could thenceforth be left unguarded. It was not the end of Anglo-American hostility, but the agreement marked the advent of an era of mutual trust. The conclusion of the War of 1812, which has sometimes been called the Second War of American Independence, marked a historical cycle. It resulted in a pacification of the old feelings of pain and resentment against Great Britain and its people—still for many Americans a kind of paternal relationship. And, by freeing them of anxieties on this front, it also freed Americans to look to the West.

FOUNDING FATHERS

The Founding Fathers were the most prominent statesmen of America's Revolutionary generation, responsible for the successful war for colonial independence from Great Britain, the liberal ideas celebrated in the Declaration of Independence, and the republican form of government defined in the United States Constitution. While there are no agreed-upon criteria for inclusion, membership in this select group customarily requires conspicuous contributions at one or both of the foundings of the United States: during the American Revolution, when independence was won, or during the Constitutional Convention, when nationhood was achieved.

Although the list of members can expand and contract in response to political pressures and ideological prejudices of the moment, the following 10, presented alphabetically, represent the "gallery of greats" that has stood the test of time: John Adams, Samuel Adams, Benjamin Franklin, Alexander Hamilton, Patrick Henry, Thomas Jefferson, James Madison, John Marshall, George Mason, and George Washington. There is a nearly unanimous consensus that George Washington was the Foundingest Father of them all.

THE DEBATE

Within the broader world of popular opinion in the United States, the Founding Fathers are often accorded near mythical status as demigods who occupy privileged locations on the slopes of some American version of Mount Olympus. Within the narrower world of the academy, however, opinion is more divided. In general, scholarship at the end of the 20th century and the beginning of the 21st has focused more on ordinary and "inarticulate" Americans in the late 18th century, the periphery of the social scene rather than the centre. And much of the scholarly work focusing on the Founders has emphasized their failures more than their successes, primarily their failure to end slavery or reach a sensible accommodation with the Native Americans.

The very term "Founding Fathers" has also struck some scholars as inherently sexist, verbally excluding women from a prominent role in the founding. Such influential women as Abigail Adams, Dolley Madison, and Mercy Otis Warren made significant contributions that merit attention, despite the fact that the Founding Fathers label obscures their role.

ABIGAIL ADAMS

Abigail Adams (née Abigail Smith) was born on November 22, 1744, in Weymouth, Massachusetts, and died on October 28, 1818, in Quincy, Massachusetts. She was the American first lady (1797–1801), the wife of John Adams, second president of the United States, and mother of John Quincy Adams, sixth president of the United States. Furthermore, she was a prolific letter writer whose correspondence gives an intimate and vivid portrayal of life in the young republic.

Born to William Smith, a Congregational minister, and Elizabeth Quincy Smith, Abigail was the second of four children. Educated entirely at home, she read widely in her father's large library, and the constant flow of interesting, intelligent, and well-educated guests at the Smith home turned her into a learned, witty young woman. For her introduction to great literature, she credited her brother-in-law, Richard Cranch.

Abigail's plans to marry John Adams, a Harvard-educated lawyer nine years her senior, did not gain the immediate approval of Smith, who considered a lawyer's prospects inadequate. When they married on October 25, 1764, the bride's father, who performed the ceremony, amused the guests by citing a passage from the Book of Luke: "John came neither eating bread nor drinking wine and some say he has a devil in him." During the first 10 years of their marriage Abigail gave birth to five children, including a daughter who died in infancy and John Quincy Adams.

She managed the second decade of her marriage on her own, as John participated in the colonial struggle for independence as a member of the Continental Congress and later as a representative of his country in France. Their correspondence during these years, especially when added to the spirited letters penned earlier during their courtship, provides a rich account of their activities and thinking as well as their love and devotion to each other. It is from these letters that historians, including the Adamses' grandson Charles Francis Adams, have concluded that Abigail played a significant role in her husband's career, particularly in managing the family farm and his business affairs. Because of her, the Adamses avoided the financial ruin that befell some other early presidents, such as Thomas Jefferson, after they left office.

As the revolutionary spirit swept through the colonies, Abigail firmly supported the movement for independence. In March 1776, when her husband prepared to gather with his colleagues to write a statement of principles that would soon be adopted by the Continental Congress as the Declaration of Independence, she asked him to "remember the ladies and be more generous and favourable to them than your ancestors." Although this letter has often been cited, correctly, as evidence of her fervent desire for women's rights, she did not champion, then or later, the right of women to vote, a position virtually unheard of at the time. She did, however, strongly support a woman's right to education, and in 1778 she wrote her husband that "you need not be told how much female education is neglected, nor how fashionable it has been to ridicule female learning." She also favoured the abolition of slavery.

In 1784 Abigail joined her husband in Europe, when he began serving as American minister to Britain. Her letters from Paris and London contain descriptive musings on British royalty, French customs, and the superiority of the quiet life of an American farmer. She wrote in early 1788 that she much preferred her "own little farm" to "the court of Saint James's where I seldom meet with characters so inoffensive as my Hens and chickings." Later that year the Adamses returned to the United States; when John assumed the vice presidency in 1789, Abigail divided her time between the capital city (first New York City and then, in 1790, Philadelphia) and the family home in Massachusetts. She missed her husband's

(continued on the next page)

ABIGAIL ADAMS (CONTINUED)

presidential inauguration in March 1797 in order to care for his sick mother, and during his presidency she often stayed in Massachusetts to look after family matters.

As first lady, she kept a rigorous daily schedule, rising at 5:00 AM to manage a busy household and receive callers for two hours each day. Unlike Martha Washington, who had been a gracious hostess but avoided all political discussions, Abigail involved herself in the most interesting debates of the day. As the two major political factions, the Federalists and the Anti-Federalists (later the Jeffersonian Republicans), developed into political parties in the 1790s, she pointed out her husband's friends and foes in both groups. About Alexander Hamilton, who along with Adams was a leading Federalist, she wrote that she saw in his eyes "the very devil . . . lasciviousness itself." She judged Albert Gallatin, a Republican opponent of her husband, "sly, artfull . . . insidious." Her critics objected that the wife of the president should not insinuate herself in political discussions; Gallatin wrote, "She is Mrs. President not of the United States but of a faction . . . It is not right."

In November 1800, just as the election that denied John Adams a second term as president was being held, Abigail oversaw the Adamses' move from Philadelphia to the newly constructed presidential mansion in Washington, D.C. Her letters to family members showed her displeasure at finding the building roughly finished and unfurnished, but she warned her daughter not to reveal her thoughts, since people would think her ungrateful. On New Year's Day 1801 she opened the mansion, soon to be known as the White House, to visitors, continuing a tradition begun by the Washingtons and maintained by every subsequent first lady until 1933.

After leaving office, Abigail and John retired to their home in Massachusetts. She continued a lively correspondence with many people and even resumed writing to Thomas Jefferson, from whom she had been estranged as a result of political differences. She died in October 1818 and was buried in the First Church of Quincy; her husband, who died in 1826, was buried beside her.

Until the 20th century few first ladies shared Abigail Adams's interest in politics or in the treatment of government leaders by the press. She vigorously objected to what she considered inaccurate reporting on her husband and son. But she was not altogether surprised by the "lies [and] Falshoods," writing in 1797 to her sister that she "expected to be vilified and abused, with my whole family." Although her approach to the office of first lady was in many ways advanced, her fame rests primarily on her thousands of letters, which form an eloquent and evocative description of her life and times.

ABIGAIL ADAMS MANAGED THE FAMILY FARM AS WELL AS JOHN'S BUSINESS AFFAIRS WHILE HE WAS AWAY. SHE ENJOYED A LIVELY POLITICAL DISCUSSION AS WELL.

As a result, the Founding Fathers label that originated in the 19th century as a quasi-religious and nearly reverential designation has become a more controversial term in the 21st. Any assessment of America's founding generation has become a conversation about the core values embodied in the political institutions of the United States, which are alternatively celebrated as the wellspring of democracy and a triumphant liberal legacy or demonized as the source of American arrogance, racism, and imperialism.

For at least two reasons, the debate over its Founders occupies a special place in America's history that has no parallel in the history of any European nation-state. First, the United States was not founded on a common ethnicity, language, or religion that could be taken for granted as the primal source of national identity. Instead, it was founded on a set of beliefs and convictions, what Thomas Jefferson described as self-evident truths, that were proclaimed in 1776 and then embedded in the Bill of Rights of the Constitution. To become an American citizen is not a matter of bloodlines or genealogy but rather a matter of endorsing and embracing the values established at the founding, which accords the men who invented these values a special significance. Second, the American system of jurisprudence links all landmark constitutional decisions to the language of the Constitution itself and often to the "original intent" of the framers. Once again, this legal tradition gives the American Founders an abiding relevance in current discussions of foreign and domestic policy that would be inconceivable in most European countries.

Finally, in part because so much always seems to be at stake whenever the Founding Fathers enter any historical conversation, the debate over their achievement and legacy tends

Among his many achievements, Thomas Jefferson drafted the U.S. Declaration of Independence and served as the first secretary of state (1789–94), the second vice president (1797–1801), and the third president (1801–09).

MERCY OTIS WARREN

Mercy Otis Warren (née Mercy Otis) was an American poet, dramatist, and historian whose proximity to political leaders and critical national events gives particular value to her writing on the American Revolutionary period. She is considered by some to be the first American woman to write primarily for the public, rather than for herself.

Mercy Otis was born to a prosperous Cape Cod family. One of her brothers was the political activist and firebrand James Otis, who was early involved in events leading to the American Revolution. She received no formal schooling but managed to absorb something of an education from her uncle, the Rev. Jonathan Russell, who tutored her brothers and allowed her to study by their side in all subjects except Latin and Greek. In 1754 she married James Warren, a merchant and farmer who went on to serve in the Massachusetts state legislature (1766–78), and bore five children. Because of her husband's political associations, Warren was personally acquainted with most of the leaders of the Revolution and was continually at or near the centre of events for more than two decades, from the Stamp Act crisis of 1765 to the establishment of the federal republic in 1789.

After her brother James was brutally beaten by colonial revenue officers in 1769, Warren was increasingly drawn to political activism and hosted protest meetings at her home that resulted in the organization of the Committees of Correspondence. Combining her unique vantage point and fervent beliefs with a talent for writing, she then became both a poet and a historian of the Revolutionary era, beginning with a trio of scathingly polemical, or controversial, plays in verse that were published serially in a Boston newspaper. *The Adulateur* (1772) foretold the War of Revolution through the actions of Rapatio, a haughty, imperious official obviously modeled on Massachusetts's royal governor, Thomas Hutchinson. *The Defeat,* also featuring Rapatio, followed a year later, and in 1775 Warren published *The Group,* a satire conjecturing what would happen if the British king abrogated the Massachusetts charter of rights. The anonymously published prose dramas *The Blockheads* (1776) and *The Motley Assembly* (1779), no less acerbic, or cutting, are also attributed to her.

As the young United States, and Massachusetts in particular, began to move in a Federalist direction following the war, Warren remained steadfastly Republican. In 1788 she published *Observations on the New Constitution,* detailing her opposition to the document on account of its emphasis on a strong central government. Warren maintained social and political correspondences with her friends John and Abigail Adams. She wrote the latter about her belief that the relegation of women to minor concerns reflected not their inferior intellect but the inferior opportunities offered them to develop their capacities. In 1790 she published *Poems, Dramatic and*

MERCY OTIS WARREN WROTE POEMS, DRAMA, AND HISTORY—SOME OF WHICH WERE CONTROVERSIAL AND OUTRIGHT SCATHING—FOR THE PUBLIC TO READ.

(continued on the next page)

MERCY OTIS WARREN (CONTINUED)

Miscellaneous, a collection of her works that contained two new plays, *The Sack of Rome* and *The Ladies of Castille*. In 1805 Warren completed a three-volume history titled *A History of the Rise, Progress, and Termination of the American Revolution*. The work deliberately avoided dull accounts of "military havoc" in favour of knowledgeable comments on the important personages of the day, which remain especially useful. Its marginalizing and sharply critical treatment of John Adams led to a heated correspondence and a breach in Warren's friendship with the Adamses that lasted until 1812.

to assume a hyperbolic shape. It is as if an electromagnetic field surrounds the discussion, driving the debate toward mutually exclusive appraisals. In much the same way that adolescents view their parents, the Founders are depicted as heroic icons or despicable villains, demigods or devils, the creators of all that is right or all that is wrong with American society. In recent years the Founder whose reputation has been tossed most dramatically across this swoonish arc is Thomas Jefferson, simultaneously the author of the most lyrical rendition of the American promise to the world and the most explicit assertion of the supposed biological inferiority of African Americans.

Since the late 1990s a surge of new books on the Founding Fathers, several of which have enjoyed surprising commercial and critical success, has begun to break free of the hyperbolic pattern and generate an adult rather than adolescent conversation in which a sense of irony and paradox replaces the old moralistic categories. This recent scholarship is heavily dependent on the massive editorial projects, ongoing since the 1960s, that have produced a level of documentation on the American Founders that is more comprehensive and detailed than the account of any political elite in recorded history.

While this enormous avalanche of historical evidence bodes well for a more nuanced and sophisticated interpretation of the founding generation, the debate is likely to retain a special edge for most Americans. As long as the United States endures as a republican government established in the late 18th century, all Americans are living the legacy of that creative moment and therefore cannot escape its grand and tragic implications. And because the American Founders were real men, not fictional legends like Romulus and Remus of Rome or King Arthur of England, they will be unable to bear the impossible burdens that Americans reflexively, perhaps inevitably, need to impose upon them.

THE ACHIEVEMENT

Given the overheated character of the debate, perhaps it is prudent to move toward less contested and more factual terrain, where it is possible to better understand what the fuss is all about. What, in the end, did the Founding Fathers manage to do? Once both the inflated and judgmental rhetorics are brushed aside, what did they achieve?

At the most general level, they created the first modern nation-state based on liberal principles. These include the democratic principle that political sovereignty in any government resides in the citizenry rather than in a divinely sanctioned monarchy; the capitalistic principle that economic productivity depends upon the release of individual energies in the marketplace rather than on state-sponsored policies; the moral principle that the individual, not the society or the state, is the sovereign unit in the political equation; and the judicial principle that all citizens are equal before the law. Moreover, this liberal formula has become the preferred political recipe for success in the modern world, vanquishing the European monarchies in the 19th century and the totalitarian regimes of Germany, Japan, and the Soviet Union in the 20th century.

More specifically, the Founding Fathers managed to defy conventional wisdom in four unprecedented achievements: first, they won a war for colonial independence against the most powerful military and economic power in the world; second, they established the first large-scale republic in the modern world; third, they invented political parties that institutionalized the concept of a legitimate opposition; and fourth, they established the principle of the legal separation of church and state, though it took several decades for that principle to be implemented in all the states. Finally, all these achievements were won without recourse to the guillotine or the firing squad, which is to say without the violent purges that accompanied subsequent revolutions in France, Russia, and China. This was the overarching accomplishment that the British philosopher Alfred Lord North Whitehead had in mind when he observed that there were only two instances in the history of Western civilization when the political elite of an emerging empire behaved as well as one could reasonably expect: the first was Rome under Augustus, and the second was the United States under the Founding Fathers.

THE FAILURE

Slavery was incompatible with the values of the American Revolution, and all the prominent members of the Revolutionary generation acknowledged that fact. In three important areas they acted on this conviction: first, by ending the slave trade in 1808; second, by passing legislation in all the states north of the Potomac River, which put slavery on the road to ultimate extinction; and third, by prohibiting the expansion of slavery into the Northwest Territory. But in all the states south of the Potomac, where some nine-tenths of the slave population resided, they failed to act. Indeed, by insisting that slavery was a matter of state rather than federal jurisdiction, the Founding Fathers implicitly removed the slavery question from the national agenda. This decision had catastrophic consequences, for it permitted the enslaved population to grow in size eightfold (from 500,000 in 1775 to 4,000,000 in 1860), mostly by natural reproduction, and to spread throughout all the southern states east of the Mississippi River. And at least in retrospect, the Founders' failure to act decisively before the slave population swelled so dramatically rendered the slavery question insoluble by any means short of civil war.

There were at least three underlying reasons for this tragic failure. First, many of the Founders mistakenly believed that slavery would die a natural death, that decisive action was unnecessary because slavery would not be able to compete successfully with the wage labour of free individuals. They did not foresee the cotton gin and the subsequent expansion of the "Cotton Kingdom." Second, all the early efforts to place slavery on the national agenda prompted a threat of secession by the states of the Deep South (South Carolina and Georgia were the two states that actually threatened to secede, though Virginia might very well have chosen to join them if the matter came to a head), a threat especially potent during the fragile phase of the early American republic. While most of the Founders regarded slavery as a malignant cancer on the body politic, they also believed that any effort to remove it surgically would in all likelihood kill the young nation in the cradle. Finally, all conversations about abolishing slavery were haunted by the spectre of a free African American population, most especially in those states south of the Potomac where in some locations blacks actually outnumbered whites. None of the Founding Fathers found it possible to imagine a biracial American society, an idea that in point of fact did not achieve broad acceptance in the United States until the middle of the 20th century.

Given these prevalent convictions and attitudes, slavery was that most un-American item, an inherently intractable and insoluble problem. As Jefferson so famously put it, the Founders held "the wolfe by the ears" and could neither subdue him nor afford to let him go. Virtually all the Founding Fathers went to their graves realizing that slavery, no matter how intractable, would become the largest and most permanent stain on their legacy. And when Abraham Lincoln eventually made the decision that, at terrible cost, ended slavery forever, he did so in the name of the Founders.

The other tragic failure of the Founders, almost as odious as the failure to end slavery, was the inability to implement a just policy toward the indigenous inhabitants of the North American continent. In 1783, the year the British surrendered control of the eastern third of North America in the Peace of Paris, there were approximately 100,000 American Indians living between the Alleghenies and the Mississippi. The first census (1790) revealed that there were also 100,000 white settlers living west of the Alleghenies, swelling in size every year (by 1800 they would number 500,000) and moving relentlessly westward. The inevitable collision between these two peoples posed the strategic and ultimately moral question: How could the legitimate rights of the Indian population be reconciled with the demographic tidal wave building to the east?

In the end, they could not. Although the official policy of Indian removal east of the Mississippi was not formally announced and implemented until 1830, the seeds of that policy—what one historian has called "the seeds of extinction"— were planted during the founding era, most especially during the presidency of Thomas Jefferson (1801–09).

One genuine effort to avoid that outcome was made in 1790 during the presidency of George Washington. The Treaty of New York with the Creek tribes of the early southwest proposed a new model for American policy toward the Indians, declaring that they should be regarded not as a conquered people with no legal rights but rather as a collection of sovereign nations. Indian policy was therefore a branch of foreign policy, and all treaties were solemn commitments by the federal government not subject to challenge by any state or private corporation. Washington envisioned a series of American Indian enclaves or homelands east of the Mississippi whose borders would be guaranteed under federal law, protected by federal troops, and bypassed by the flood of white settlers. But, as it soon became clear, the federal government lacked the resources in money and manpower to make Washington's vision a reality. And the very act of claiming executive power to create an Indian protectorate prompted charges of monarchy, the most potent political epithet of the age. Washington, who was accustomed to getting his way, observed caustically that nothing short of "a Chinese Wall" could protect the Native American tribes from the relentless expansion of white settlements. Given the surging size of the white population, it is difficult to imagine how the story could have turned out differently.

THE EXPLANATIONS

Meanwhile, the more mythical rendition of the Founders, which continues to dominate public opinion outside the groves of academe, presumes that their achievements dwarf their failures so completely that the only question worth asking is: How did they do it? More specifically, how did this backwoods province on the western rim of the Atlantic world, far removed from the epicentres of learning and culture in London and Paris, somehow produce thinkers and ideas that transformed the landscape of modern politics?

Two historical explanations have been offered, each focusing on the special conditions present in Revolutionary America favourable to the creation of leadership. The first explanation describes the founding era as a unique moment that was "postaristocratic" and "predemocratic." In the former sense, American society was more open to talent than England or the rest of Europe, where hereditary bloodlines were essential credentials for entry into public life. The Founders comprised what Jefferson called "a natural aristocracy," meaning a political elite based on merit rather than genealogy, thus permitting men of impoverished origins such as Alexander Hamilton and Benjamin Franklin, who would have languished in obscurity in

London, to reach the top tier. In the latter (i.e., predemocratic) sense, the Founders were a self-conscious elite unburdened by egalitarian assumptions. Their constituency was not "the people" but "the public," which they regarded as the long-term interest of the citizenry that they—the Founders—had been chosen to divine. Living between the assumptions of an aristocratic and a democratic world without belonging fully to either, the Founders maximized the advantages of both.

The second explanation focuses on the crisis-driven pressures that forced latent talent to the surface. When Jefferson concluded the Declaration of Independence by proclaiming that all the signers of the document were wagering "our lives, our fortunes, and our sacred honor" on the cause, he was engaging in more than a rhetorical flourish. For example, when Washington departed Mount Vernon for Philadelphia in May 1775, he presumed that the British would burn his estate to the ground once war was declared. An analogous gamble was required in 1787–88 to endorse the unprecedented viability of a large-scale American republic. The founding era, according to this explanation, was a propitious all-or-nothing moment in which only those blessed with uncommon conviction about the direction in which history was headed could survive the test. The severe and unforgiving political gauntlet the Founders were required to run eliminated lukewarm patriots and selected for survival only those leaders with the hard residue of unalloyed resolve.

This was probably what Ralph Waldo Emerson meant when he cautioned the next generation of aspiring American leaders to avoid measuring themselves against the Founders. They had the incalculable advantage, Emerson observed, of being "present at the creation" and thus seeing God "face to face." All who came after them could only see him secondhand.

A DIVERSE COLLECTIVE

Thus far the identity, achievements, and failures of the Founding Fathers have been considered as if they were the expression of a composite personality with a singular orientation. But this is wildly misleading. The term "Founding Fathers" is a plural noun, which in turn means that the face of the American Revolution is a group portrait. To be sure, Washington was *primus inter pares*, or first among equals, within the founding generation, generally regarded, then and thereafter, as "the indispensable figure." But unlike subsequent revolutions in France, Russia, and China, where a single person came to embody the meaning of the revolutionary movement—Napoleon I, Vladimir Ilich Lenin/Joseph Stalin, Mao Zedong—the revolutionary experience in the United States had multiple faces and multiple meanings that managed to coexist without ever devolving into a unitary embodiment of authority. If one of the distinctive contributions of the American political tradition was a pluralistic conception of governance, its primal source was the pluralistic character of the founding generation itself.

All the Founders agreed that American independence from Great Britain was nonnegotiable and that whatever government was established in lieu of British rule must be republican in character. Beyond this elemental consensus, however, there was widespread disagreement, which surfaced most dramatically in the debate over ratification of the Constitution (1787–88). Two prominent Founders, Patrick Henry and George Mason, opposed ratification, claiming that the Constitution created a central government that only replicated the arbitrary power of the British monarchy and Parliament. The highly partisan politics of the 1790s further exposed the several fault lines within the founding elite. The Federalists, led by Washington, John Adams, and Hamilton, were opposed by the Republicans, led by Jefferson and James Madison. They disagreed over the proper allocation of federal and state power over domestic policy, the response to the French Revolution, the constitutionality of the Bank of the United States, and the bedrock values of American foreign policy. These disagreements often assumed a hyperbolic tone because nothing less than the "true meaning" of the American Revolution seemed at stake. In what became the capstone correspondence of the Revolutionary generation, Adams and Jefferson both went to their Maker on July 4, 1826, arguing quite poignantly about their incompatible versions of the Revolutionary legacy.

The ideological and even temperamental diversity within the elite leadership group gave the American founding a distinctly argumentative flavour that made all convictions, no matter how cherished, subject to abiding scrutiny that, like history itself, became an argument without end. And much like the doctrine of checks and balances in the Constitution, the enshrinement of argument created a permanent collision of juxtaposed ideas and interests that generated a dynamic and wholly modern version of political stability.

RELIGION AND POSTERITY

Although the Declaration of Independence mentioned "Nature's God" and the "Creator," the Constitution made no reference to a divine being, Christian or otherwise, and the First Amendment explicitly forbade the establishment of any official

DOLLEY MADISON

Dolley Madison (née Dolley Payne and also known as Dolley Todd or Dolly) was the first lady (1809–17), the wife of James Madison, fourth president of the United States. Raised in the plain style of her Quaker family, she was renowned for her charm, warmth, and ingenuity. Her popularity as manager of the White House made that task a responsibility of every first lady who followed.

Dolley was one of eight children of John Payne, a merchant, and Mary Coles Payne. Soon after her birth, her father's business fell on hard times and the family moved to eastern Virginia, where they were active members of the Society of Friends. When she was 15 her family moved to Philadelphia, where Dolley married a young lawyer, John Todd, in 1790. The couple had two children, but in 1793 her youngest son and husband died during an epidemic of yellow fever, widowing Dolley at 25.

A few months later Aaron Burr, then a United States senator from New Jersey, introduced Dolley to James Madison, who was 17 years her senior; though a small man physically he was a towering political figure. There was a mutual, immediate, and strong attraction between James and Dolley, and they wed on September 15, 1794, at her sister's home in Virginia. Because her husband was Episcopalian, however, the Quakers disowned her. Soon after their marriage, accompanied by her son, the Madisons moved to Philadelphia, then the nation's capital, where James served as a member of the House of Representatives. During the presidency of John Adams (1797–1801), the Madisons lived on James's estate, Montpellier (now Montpelier), in Virginia. Soon after the election of Thomas Jefferson in 1800, they relocated to Washington, D.C., where James served as secretary of state and Dolley assisted the widowed Jefferson as hostess at official events, giving her ample preparation for her future role as first lady.

The first president's wife to preside over the White House for any significant amount of time, Dolley Madison set many precedents. She established the tradition that the mansion would reflect the first lady's tastes and ideas about entertaining. With the help of Benjamin Latrobe, architect and surveyor of public buildings, she decorated and furnished the house so that it was both elegant and comfortable. Unfortunately, not many Americans had the chance to see it before the British burned the mansion in August 1814 during the War of 1812. Dolley underscored the first lady's responsibility for caring for the mansion and its contents when she directed the removal and safe storage of precious holdings, including the famous Gilbert Stuart portrait of George Washington that still hangs in the East Room.

DOLLEY MADISON'S MANAGEMENT OF THE WHITE HOUSE WAS SO EFFECTIVE AND INGENIOUS THAT EVERY FIRST LADY TO FOLLOW HER HAS DECORATED THE PRESIDENTIAL HOME IN HER OWN TASTE AND STYLE.

As hostess, Dolley Madison carefully balanced two competing traditions in the new nation: the democratic emphasis on equal treatment and the elitist notion that the president's house was the province of the privileged few. At weekly receptions she opened

(*continued on the next page*)

DOLLEY MADISON (CONTINUED)

the doors to virtually anyone who wanted to come and then moved among the guests, greeting all with charming ease. In her stylish turbans and imported clothes, she became enormously popular and much imitated. Although most Americans approved, she did have her critics, including Elijah Mills, a senator from Massachusetts, who complained that she mixed "all classes of people . . . greasy boots and silk stockings."

Although she eschewed taking public stands on controversial issues, Dolley had a shrewd political sense and cultivated her husband's enemies as carefully as his friends. When President Madison dismissed his secretary of state, Robert Smith, she invited him to dinner; when he failed to accept she went to call on him personally. In the election of 1812, when many Americans complained that Madison had led them into an unnecessary war, she used her invitation lists to win him favour and a second term, according to some historians.

She insisted on visiting the household of every new representative or senator, a task that proved very time-consuming as the nation grew and the number of congressmen increased. Because many representatives chose to bring their families to Washington, dozens of households expected a call from the president's wife. Her successors found the practice too burdensome and stopped it.

Dolley Madison enjoyed a happy marriage; different as she and her husband were in personality, they doted on each other. However, her relationship with her son, John Payne Todd, was a different matter. He spent money recklessly and expected his mother to cover his debts and losses.

When James's second term ended in 1817, he and Dolley moved back to Montpellier, where they lived until his death in 1836.

James's last decades were not prosperous, and the debts of young Payne Todd depleted the family's resources. To supplement Dolley's income after James's death, a sympathetic and grateful Congress appropriated $30,000 to purchase the Madison papers.

In 1837 Dolley moved back to Washington. Living in a home opposite the White House, she was the nation's most prestigious hostess. Presidents and social leaders called on her, and she was a frequent White House guest. But her profligate son continued to try her patience and deplete her purse. In 1842 she traveled to New York City to arrange a loan from the wealthy fur magnate John Jacob Astor, and Congress came to her aid once more by agreeing to buy the remaining Madison papers for $25,000, but only on the condition that the money be placed in trust so that her son could not get it.

When Dolley Madison died in 1849 she was one of the most popular figures in Washington and the nation's favourite first lady. At her funeral President Zachary Taylor, his cabinet, the diplomatic corps, and members of Congress lined up to pay their respects. She was buried beside James Madison at a family plot near Montpelier.

church or creed. There is also a story, probably apocryphal, that Franklin's proposal to call in a chaplain to offer a prayer when a particularly controversial issue was being debated in the Constitutional Convention prompted Hamilton to observe that he saw no reason to call in foreign aid. If there is a clear legacy bequeathed by the Founders, it is the insistence that religion is a private matter in which the state should not interfere.

In recent decades Christian advocacy groups, prompted by motives that have been questioned by some, have felt a powerful urge to enlist the Founding Fathers in their respective congregations. But recovering the spiritual convictions of the

Founders, in all their messy integrity, is not an easy task. Once again, diversity is the dominant pattern. Franklin and Jefferson were Deists, Washington harboured a pantheistic sense of Providential destiny, John Adams began as a Congregationalist and ended as a Unitarian, and Hamilton was a lukewarm Anglican for most of his life but embraced a more actively Christian posture after his son died in a duel.

One quasi-religious conviction they all shared, however, was a discernible obsession with living on in the memory of posterity. One reason the modern editions of their papers are so monstrously large is that most of the Founders were compulsively fastidious about preserving every scrap of paper they wrote or received, all as part of a desire to leave a written record that would assure their secular immortality in the history books. (When John Adams and Jefferson discussed the possibility of a more conventional immortality, they tended to describe heaven as a place where they could resume their ongoing argument on earth.) Adams, irreverent to the end, declared that if it could ever be demonstrated conclusively that no future state existed, his advice to every man, woman, and child was to "take opium." The only afterlife that the Founders considered certain was in the memory of subsequent generations, which is to say us. In that sense, this very introduction is a testimonial to their everlasting life.

GEORGE WASHINGTON: REVOLUTIONARY LEADER

George Washington, also called the Father of His Country, was general and commander in chief of the colonial armies in the American Revolution (1775–83). He went on to become the first president of the United States (1789–97).

Washington's father, Augustine Washington, had gone to school in England, tasted seafaring life, and then settled down to manage his growing Virginia estates. His mother was Mary Ball, whom Augustine, a widower, had married early the previous year. Washington's paternal lineage had some distinction; an early forebear was described as a "gentleman," Henry VIII later gave the family lands, and its members held various offices. But family fortunes fell with the Puritan revolution in England, and John Washington, grandfather of Augustine, migrated in 1657 to Virginia. The ancestral home at Sulgrave, Northampton-shire, is maintained as a Washington memorial. Little definite information exists on any of the line until Augustine. He was an energetic, ambitious man who acquired much land, built mills, took an interest in opening iron mines, and sent his two eldest sons to England for schooling. By his first wife, Jane Butler, he had four children. By his second wife, Mary Ball, he had six. Augustine died April 12, 1743.

YOUNG GEORGE

Little is known of George Washington's early childhood, spent largely on the Ferry Farm on the Rappahannock River, opposite Fredericksburg, Virginia. Mason L. Weems's stories of the hatchet and cherry tree and of young Washington's repugnance to fighting are apocryphal efforts to fill a manifest gap. He attended school irregularly from his 7th to his 15th year, first with the local church sexton and later with a schoolmaster named Williams. Some of his schoolboy papers survive. He was fairly well trained in practical mathematics—gauging, several types of mensuration, and some trigonometry that was useful in surveying. He studied geography, possibly had a little Latin, and certainly read some of *The Spectator* and other English classics. The copybook in which he transcribed at 14 a set of moral precepts, or *Rules of Civility and Decent Behaviour in Company and Conversation*, was carefully preserved. His best training, however, was given him by practical men and outdoor occupations, not by books. He mastered tobacco growing and stock raising, and early in his teens he was sufficiently familiar with surveying to plot the fields about him.

At his father's death, the 11-year-old boy became the ward of his eldest half brother, Lawrence, a man of fine character who gave him wise and affectionate care. Lawrence inherited the beautiful estate of Little Hunting Creek, which had been granted to the original settler, John Washington, and which Augustine had done much since 1738 to develop. Lawrence married Anne (Nancy) Fairfax, daughter of Col. William Fairfax, a cousin and agent of Lord Fairfax and one of the chief proprietors of the region. Lawrence also built a house and named the 2,500-acre (1,000-hectare) holding Mount Vernon in honour of the admiral under whom he had served in the siege of Cartagena. Living

MOUNT VERNON IN FAIRFAX COUNTY, VA., WAS NAMED BY GEORGE WASHINGTON'S OLDEST HALF-BROTHER, LAWRENCE. IT WOULD BE WASHINGTON'S HOME AND FINAL RESTING PLACE.

there chiefly with Lawrence (though he spent some time near Fredericksburg with his other half brother, Augustine [called Austin]), George entered a more spacious and polite world. Anne Fairfax Washington was a woman of charm, grace, and culture; Lawrence had brought from his English school and naval service much knowledge and experience. A valued neighbour and relative, George William Fairfax, whose large estate, Belvoir, was about 4 miles (6 km) distant, and other relatives by marriage, the Carlyles of Alexandria, helped form George's mind and manners.

WASHINGTON TOOK MANAGEMENT OF MOUNT VERNON SERIOUSLY. ALTHOUGH THIS LITHOGRAPH MIGHT BE A SENTIMENTALIZED VIEW OF FARM LIFE, WASHINGTON REFUSED TO SELL SLAVES AND RISK BREAKING UP FAMILIES.

The youth turned first to surveying as a profession. Lord Fairfax, a middle-aged bachelor who owned more than 5,000,000 acres (2,000,000 hectares) in northern Virginia and the Shenandoah Valley, came to America in 1746 to live with his cousin George William at Belvoir and to look after his properties. Two years later he sent to the Shenandoah Valley a party to survey and plot his lands to make regular tenants of the squatters moving in from Pennsylvania. With the official surveyor of Prince William county in charge, Washington went along as assistant. The 16-year-old lad kept a disjointed diary of the trip, which shows skill in observation. He describes the discomfort of sleeping under "one thread Bear blanket with double its Weight of Vermin such as Lice Fleas & c"; an encounter with an Indian war party bearing a scalp; the Pennsylvania-German emigrants, "as ignorant a set of people as the Indians they would never speak English but when spoken to they speak all Dutch"; and the serving of roast wild turkey on "a Large Chip," for "as for dishes we had none."

The following year (1749), aided by Lord Fairfax, Washington received an appointment as official surveyor of Culpeper county, and for more than two years he was kept almost constantly busy. Surveying not only in Culpeper but also in Frederick and Augusta counties, he made journeys far beyond the Tidewater region into the western wilderness. The experience taught him resourcefulness and endurance and toughened him in both body and mind. Coupled with Lawrence's ventures in land, it also gave him an interest in western development that endured throughout his life. He was always disposed to speculate in western holdings and to view favourably projects for colonizing the West, and he greatly resented the limitations that the crown in time laid on the westward movement. In 1752 Lord Fairfax determined to take up his final residence in the Shenandoah Valley and settled there in a log hunting lodge, which he called Greenway Court after a Kentish manor of his family's. There Washington was sometimes entertained and had access to a small library that Fairfax had begun accumulating at Oxford.

The years 1751–52 marked a turning point in Washington's life, for they placed him in control of Mount Vernon. Lawrence, stricken by tuberculosis, went to Barbados in 1751 for his health, taking George along. From this sole journey beyond the present borders of the United States, Washington returned with the light scars of an attack of smallpox. In July of the next year, Lawrence died, making George executor and residuary heir of his estate should his daughter, Sarah, die without issue. As she died within two months, Washington at age 20 became head of one of the best Virginia estates. He always thought farming the "most delectable" of pursuits. "It is honorable," he wrote, "it is amusing, and, with superior judgment, it is profitable." And, of all the spots for farming, he thought Mount Vernon the best. "No estate in United America," he assured an English correspondent, "is more pleasantly situated than this." His greatest pride in later days was to be regarded as the first farmer of the land.

He gradually increased the estate until it exceeded 8,000 acres (3,000 hectares). He enlarged the house in 1760 and made further enlargements and improvements on the house and its landscaping in 1784–86. He also tried to keep abreast of the latest scientific advances.

For the next 20 years the main background of Washington's life was the work and society of Mount Vernon. He gave diligent attention to the rotation of crops, fertilization of the soil, and the management of livestock. He had to manage the

18 slaves that came with the estate and others he bought later; by 1760 he had paid taxes on 49 slaves—though he strongly disapproved of the institution and hoped for some mode of abolishing it. At the time of his death, more than 300 slaves were housed in the quarters on his property. He had been unwilling to sell slaves lest families be broken up, even though the increase in their numbers placed a burden on him for their upkeep and gave him a larger force of workers than he required, especially after he gave up the cultivation of tobacco. In his will, he bequeathed the slaves in his possession to his wife and ordered that upon her death they be set free, declaring also that the young, the aged, and the infirm among them "shall be comfortably cloathed & fed by my heirs." Still, this accounted for only about half the slaves on his property. The other half, owned by his wife, were entailed to the Custis estate, so that on her death they were destined to pass to her heirs. However, she freed all the slaves in 1800 after his death.

For diversion Washington was fond of riding, fox hunting, and dancing, of such theatrical performances as he could reach, and of duck hunting and sturgeon fishing. He liked billiards and cards and not only subscribed to racing associations but also ran his own horses in races. In all outdoor pursuits, from wrestling to colt breaking, he excelled. A friend of the 1750s describes him as "straight as an Indian, measuring six feet two inches in his stockings"; as very muscular and broad-shouldered but, though large-boned, weighing only 175 pounds; and as having long arms and legs. His penetrating blue-gray eyes were overhung by heavy brows, his nose was large and straight, and his mouth was large and firmly closed. "His movements and gestures are graceful, his walk majestic, and he is a splendid horseman." He soon became prominent in community affairs, was an active member and later vestryman of the Episcopal church, and as early as 1755 expressed a desire to stand for the Virginia House of Burgesses.

PREREVOLUTIONARY POLITICS

Washington's contented life was interrupted by the rising storm in imperial affairs. The British ministry, facing a heavy postwar debt, high home taxes, and continued military costs in America, decided in 1764 to obtain revenue from the colonies. Up to that time, Washington, though regarded by associates, in Col. John L. Peyton's words, as "a young man of an extraordinary and exalted character," had shown no signs of personal greatness and few signs of interest in state affairs. The Proclamation of 1763 interdicting settlement beyond the Alleghenies irked him, for he was interested in the Ohio Company, the Mississippi Company, and other speculative western ventures. He nevertheless played a silent part in the House of Burgesses and was a thoroughly loyal subject.

But he was present when Patrick Henry introduced his resolutions against the Stamp Act in May 1765 and shortly thereafter gave token of his adherence to the cause of the colonial Whigs against the Tory ministries of England. In 1768 he told George Mason at Mount Vernon that he would take his musket on his shoulder whenever his country called him. The next spring, on April 4, 1769, he sent Mason the Philadelphia nonimportation resolutions with a letter declaring that it was necessary to resist the strokes of "our lordly masters" in England; that, courteous remonstrances to Parliament having failed, he wholly endorsed the resort to commercial warfare; and that as a last resort no man should scruple to use arms in defense of liberty. When, the following month, the royal governor of Virginia dissolved the House of Burgesses, he shared in the gathering, at the Raleigh Tavern in Williamsburg, that drew up nonimportation resolutions, and he went further than most of his neighbours in adhering to them. At that time and later he believed with most Americans that peace need not be broken.

Late in 1770 he paid a land-hunting visit to Fort Pitt, where George Croghan was maturing his plans for the proposed 14th colony of Vandalia. Washington directed his agent to locate and survey 10,000 acres adjoining the Vandalia tract, and at one time he wished to share in certain of Croghan's schemes. But the Boston Tea Party of December 1773 and the bursting of the Vandalia bubble at about the same time turned his eyes back to the East and the threatening state of Anglo-American relations. He was not a member of the Virginia committee of correspondence formed in 1773 to communicate with other colonies, but when the Virginia legislators, meeting irregularly again at the Raleigh Tavern in May 1774, called for a Continental Congress, he was present and signed the resolutions. Moreover, he was a leading member of the first provincial convention or revolutionary legislature late that summer, and to that body he made a speech that was much praised for its pithy eloquence, declaring that "I will raise one thousand men, subsist them at my own expense, and march myself at their head for the relief of Boston."

The Virginia provincial convention promptly elected Washington one of the seven delegates to the first Continental Congress. He was by this time known as a radical rather than a moderate, and in several letters of the time he opposed a continuance of petitions to the British crown, declaring that they would inevitably meet with a humiliating rejection. "Shall we after this whine and cry for relief when we have already tried it in vain?" he wrote. When the Congress met in Philadelphia on September 5, 1774, he was in his seat in full uniform, and his participation in its councils marks the beginning of his national career.

His letters of the period show that, while still utterly opposed to the idea of independence, he was determined never to submit "to the loss of those valuable rights and privileges, which are essential to the happiness of every free State, and without which life, liberty, and property are rendered totally insecure." If the ministry pushed matters to an extremity, he wrote, "more blood will be spilled on this occasion than ever before in American history." Though he served on none of the committees, he was a useful member, his advice being sought on military matters and weight being attached to his advocacy of a nonexportation as well as nonimportation agreement. He also helped to secure approval of the Suffolk Resolves, which looked toward armed resistance as a last resort and did much to harden the king's heart against America.

Returning to Virginia in November, he took command of the volunteer companies drilling there and served as chairman of the Committee of Safety in Fairfax county. Although the province contained many experienced officers and Col. William Byrd of Westover had succeeded Washington as commander in chief, the unanimity with which the Virginia troops turned to Washington was a tribute to his reputation and personality; it was understood that Virginia expected him to be its general. He was elected to the second Continental Congress at the March 1775 session of the legislature and again set out for Philadelphia.

REVOLUTIONARY LEADERSHIP

The choice of Washington as commander in chief of the military forces of all the colonies followed immediately upon the first fighting, though it was by no means inevitable and was the product of partly artificial forces. The Virginia delegates differed upon his appointment. Edmund Pendleton was, according to John Adams, "very full and clear against it," and Washington himself recommended Gen. Andrew Lewis for the post. It was chiefly the fruit of a political bargain by which New England offered Virginia the chief command as its price for the adoption and support of the New England army. This army had gathered hastily and in force about Boston immediately after the clash of British troops and American minutemen at Lexington and Concord on April 19, 1775. When the second Continental Congress met in Philadelphia on May 10, one of its first tasks was to find a permanent leadership for this force. On June 15, Washington, whose military counsel had already proved invaluable on two committees, was nominated and chosen by unanimous vote. Beyond the considerations noted, he owed being chosen to the facts that Virginia stood with Massachusetts as one of the most powerful colonies; that his appointment would augment the zeal of the Southern people; that he had gained an enduring reputation in the Braddock campaign; and that his poise, sense, and resolution had impressed all the delegates. The scene of his election, with Washington darting modestly into an adjoining room and John Hancock flushing with jealous mortification, will always impress the historical imagination; so also will the scene of July 3, 1775, when, wheeling his horse under an elm in front of the troops paraded on Cambridge common, he drew his sword and took command of the army investing Boston. News of Bunker Hill had reached him before he was a day's journey from Philadelphia, and he had expressed confidence of victory when told how the militia had fought. In accepting the command, he refused any payment beyond his expenses and called upon "every gentleman in the room" to bear witness that he disclaimed fitness for it. At once he showed characteristic decision and energy in organizing the raw volunteers, collecting provisions and munitions, and rallying Congress and the colonies to his support.

IN COMMAND

The first phase of Washington's command covered the period from July 1775 to the British evacuation of Boston in March 1776. In those eight months he imparted discipline to the army, which at maximum strength slightly exceeded 20,000; he dealt with subordinates who, as John Adams said, quarreled "like cats and dogs"; and he kept the siege vigorously alive. Having himself planned an invasion of Canada by Lake Champlain, to be entrusted to Gen. Philip Schuyler, he heartily approved of Benedict Arnold's proposal to march north along the Kennebec River in Maine and take Quebec. Giving Arnold 1,100 men, he instructed him to do everything possible to conciliate the Canadians. He was equally active in encouraging privateers to attack British commerce. As fast as means offered, he strengthened his army with ammunition and siege guns, having heavy artillery brought from Fort Ticonderoga, New York, over the frozen roads early in 1776. His position was at first precarious, for the

Charles River pierced the centre of his lines investing Boston. If the British general, Sir William Howe, had moved his 20 veteran regiments boldly up the stream, he might have pierced Washington's army and rolled either wing back to destruction. But all the generalship was on Washington's side. Seeing that Dorchester Heights, just south of Boston, commanded the city and harbour and that Howe had unaccountably failed to occupy it, he seized it on the night of March 4, 1776, placing his Ticonderoga guns in position. The British naval commander declared that he could not remain if the Americans were not dislodged, and Howe, after a storm disrupted his plans for an assault, evacuated the city on March 17. He left 200 cannons and invaluable stores of small arms and munitions. After collecting his booty, Washington hurried south to take up the defense of New York.

Washington had won the first round, but there remained five years of the war, during which the American cause was repeatedly near complete disaster. It is unquestionable that Washington's strength of character, his ability to hold the confidence of army and people and to diffuse his own courage among them, his unremitting activity, and his strong common sense constituted the chief factors in achieving American victory. He was not a great tactician: as Jefferson said later, he often "failed in the field"; he was sometimes guilty of grave military blunders, the chief being his assumption of a position on Long Island, New York, in 1776 that exposed his entire army to capture the moment it was defeated. At the outset he was painfully inexperienced, the wilderness fighting of the French war having done nothing to teach him the strategy of maneuvering whole armies. One of his chief faults was his tendency to subordinate his own judgment to that of the generals surrounding him; at every critical juncture, before Boston, before New York, before Philadelphia, and in New Jersey, he called a council of war and in almost every instance accepted its decision. Naturally bold and dashing, as he proved at Trenton, Princeton, and Germantown, he repeatedly adopted evasive and delaying tactics on the advice of his associates; however, he did succeed in keeping a strong army in existence and maintaining the flame of national spirit. When the auspicious moment arrived, he planned the rapid movements that ended the war.

One element of Washington's strength was his sternness as a disciplinarian. The army was continually dwindling and refilling, politics largely governed the selection of officers by Congress and the states, and the ill-fed, ill-clothed, ill-paid forces were often half-prostrated by sickness and ripe for mutiny. Troops from each of the three sections, New England, the middle states, and the South, showed a deplorable jealousy of the others. Washington was rigorous in breaking cowardly, inefficient, and dishonest men and boasted in front of Boston that he had "made a pretty good sort of slam among such kind of officers." Deserters and plunderers were flogged, and Washington once erected a gallows 40 feet (12 metres) high, writing, "I am determined if I can be justified in the proceeding, to hang two or three on it, as an example to others." At the same time, the commander in chief won the devotion of many of his men by his earnestness in demanding better treatment for them from Congress. He complained of their short rations, declaring once that they were forced to "eat every kind of horse food but hay."

The darkest chapter in Washington's military leadership was opened when, reaching New York in April 1776, he placed half his army, about 9,000 men, under Israel Putnam, on the perilous position of Brooklyn Heights, Long Island, where a

British fleet in the East River might cut off their retreat. He spent a fortnight in May with the Continental Congress in Philadelphia, then discussing the question of independence; though no record of his utterances exists, there can be no doubt that he advocated complete separation. His return to New York preceded but slightly the arrival of the British army under Howe, which made its main encampment on Staten Island until its whole strength of nearly 30,000 could be mobilized. On August 22, 1776, Howe moved about 20,000 men across to Gravesend Bay on Long Island. Four days later, sending the fleet under command of his brother Adm. Richard Howe to make a feint against New York City, he thrust a crushing force along feebly protected roads against the American flank. The patriots were outmaneuvered, defeated, and suffered a total loss of 5,000 men, of whom 2,000 were captured. Their whole position might have been carried by storm, but, fortunately for Washington, General Howe delayed. While the enemy lingered, Washington succeeded under cover of a dense fog in ferrying the remaining force across the East River to Manhattan, where he took up a fortified position. The British, suddenly landing on the lower part of the island, drove back the Americans in a clash marked by disgraceful cowardice on the part of troops from Connecticut and others. In a series of actions, Washington was forced northward, more than once in danger of capture, until the loss of his two Hudson River forts, one of them with 2,600 men, compelled him to retreat from White Plains across the river into New Jersey. He retired toward the Delaware River while his army melted away, until it seemed that armed resistance to the British was about to expire.

THE TRENTON-PRINCETON CAMPAIGN

It was at this darkest hour of the Revolution that Washington struck his brilliant blows at Trenton and Princeton in New Jersey, reviving the hopes and energies of the nation. Howe, believing that the American army soon would dissolve totally, retired to New York, leaving strong forces in Trenton and Burlington. Washington, at his camp west of the Delaware River, planned a simultaneous attack on both posts, using his whole command of 6,000 men. But his subordinates in charge of both wings failed him, and he was left on the night of December 25, 1776, to march on Trenton with about 2,400 men. With the help of Colonel John Glover's regiment, which was comprised of fishermen and sailors from Marblehead, Massachusetts, Washington and his troops were ferried across the Delaware River. In the dead of night and amid a blinding snowstorm, they then marched 10 miles (16 km) downstream and in the early hours of the morning caught the enemy at Trenton unaware. In less than two hours and without the loss of a single man in battle, Washington's troops defeated the Hessians, killed their commander (Johann Rall), and captured nearly 1,000 prisoners and arms and ammunition. This historic Christmas crossing proved to be a turning point in the war, and it was immortalized for posterity by Emanuel Gottlieb Leutze in his famous 1851 painting of the event. (The painting is historically inaccurate: the depicted flag is anachronistic, the boats are the wrong size and shape, and it is questionable whether Washington could have crossed the icy Delaware while standing in the manner depicted.)

ON DECEMBER 25, 1776, WHEN GEORGE WASHINGTON AND HIS CREW MADE THEIR HISTORIC, DARK, SNOWY TRIP ACROSS THE DELAWARE RIVER, THEY CHANGED THE COURSE OF THE WAR.

The immediate result of this American victory was that Gen. Charles Cornwallis hastened with about 8,000 men to Trenton, where he found Washington strongly posted behind the Assunpink Creek, skirmished with him, and decided to wait overnight "to bag the old fox." During the night, the wind shifted, the roads froze hard, and Washington was able to steal away from camp (leaving his fires deceptively burning), march around Cornwallis's rear, and fall at daybreak upon the three British regiments at Princeton. These were put to flight with a loss of 500 men, and Washington escaped with more captured munitions to a strong position at Morristown, New Jersey. The effect of these victories heartened all Americans, brought recruits flocking to camp in the spring, and encouraged foreign sympathizers with the American cause.

Thus far the important successes had been won by Washington; then battlefield success fell to others, while he was left to face popular apathy, military cabals, and the disaffection of Congress. The year 1777 was marked by the British capture of Philadelphia and the surrender of British Gen. John Burgoyne's invading army to Gen. Horatio Gates at Saratoga, New York, followed by intrigues to displace Washington from his command. Howe's main British army of 18,000 left New York by sea on July 23, 1777, and landed on August 25 in Maryland, not far below Philadelphia. Washington, despite his inferiority of force—he had only 11,000 men, mostly militia and, in the marquis de Lafayette's words, "badly armed and worse clothed"—risked a pitched battle on September 11 at the fords of Brandywine Creek, about 13 miles (21 km) north of Wilmington, Delaware. While part of the British force held the Americans engaged, General Cornwallis, with the rest, made a secret 17-mile (27-km) detour and fell with crushing effect on the American right and rear, the result being a complete defeat from which Washington was fortunate to extricate his army in fairly good order. For a time he hoped to hold the Schuylkill Fords, but the British passed them and on September 26 triumphantly marched into Philadelphia. Congress fled to the interior of Pennsylvania, and Washington, after an unsuccessful effort to repeat his stroke at Trenton against the British troops posted at Germantown, had to take up winter quarters at Valley Forge. His army, twice beaten, ill housed, and ill fed, with thousands of men "barefoot and otherwise naked," was at the point of exhaustion; it could not keep the field, for inside of a month it would have disappeared. Under these circumstances, there is nothing that better proves the true fibre of Washington's character and the courage of his soul than the unyielding persistence with which he held his strong position at Valley Forge through a winter of semistarvation, of justified grumbling by his men, of harsh public criticism, and of captious meddling by a Congress that was too weak to help him. In February Martha Washington arrived and helped to organize entertainment for the soldiers.

Washington's enemies seized the moment of his greatest weakness to give vent to an antagonism that had been nourished by sectional jealousies of North against South, by the ambition of small rivals, and by baseless accusations that he showed favouritism to such foreigners as Lafayette. The intrigues of Thomas Conway, an Irish adventurer who had served in the French army and had become an American general, enlisted Thomas Mifflin, Charles Lee, Benjamin Rush, and others in an attempt to displace Washington. General Gates appears to have been a tool of rather than a party to the plot, expecting that the chief command would devolve upon himself. A faction of

MARTHA WASHINGTON

Martha Washington (née Martha Dandridge, also called Martha Custis) was the first American first lady and is best known as the wife of George Washington, first president of the United States and commander in chief of the colonial armies during the American Revolutionary War. She set many of the standards and customs for the proper behaviour and treatment of the president's wife.

Daughter of farmers John and Frances Jones Dandridge, Martha grew up among the wealthy plantation families of the Tidewater region of eastern Virginia, and she received an education traditional for young women of her class and time, one in which domestic skills and the arts far outweighed science and mathematics. In 1749, at age 18, she married Daniel Parke Custis, who was 20 years her senior and an heir to a neighbouring plantation. During their life together she bore four children, two of whom died in infancy. Her husband's death in July 1757 made her one of the wealthiest widows in the region.

In the spring of the following year George Washington, then a young plantation owner and commander of the Virginia forces in the French and Indian War, began to court her, and their attachment grew increasingly deep. The couple married at Martha's home on January 6, 1759, and she and her children joined Washington at Mount Vernon, his plantation on the Potomac River. Washington later resented suggestions, which were undoubtedly true, that his wife's considerable property had eased his life in the early years of their marriage.

At Mount Vernon Martha became known for her graciousness and hospitality. After George was chosen to command the American forces in the Revolutionary War, Martha spent winters with him at his various military quarters, where she lived simply and encouraged other officers' wives to help in the war effort by economizing and assisting their husbands. After the war, during which her only surviving son died, Martha virtually adopted two of her grandchildren, and they substituted in many ways for the children she and George never had.

In 1789, shortly after her husband's inauguration as president of the United States, Martha joined him in New York City, then the national capital. Martha was widely hailed and often feted along the route, and she became known to Americans as "Lady Washington." The couple's rented home on Broadway also served as the president's office,

UNLIKE TODAY'S FIRST LADIES, MARTHA WASHINGTON DID NOT TAKE STANDS ON PUBLIC ISSUES. SHE WAS WELL KNOWN (AND SOMETIMES CRITIQUED) FOR LAVISH HOSPITALITY.

exposing her to her husband's callers and drawing her into political discussions more than would have been the case had home and office been separated. When Philadelphia became the seat of government in 1790 and the Washingtons moved to a house on High Street, Martha's hospitality became even more elaborate. The first lady took no stands on public issues, but she was criticized

(*continued on the next page*)

MARTHA WASHINGTON (CONTINUED)

by some for entertaining on a scale too opulent for a republican government, and she was only too glad to retire to Mount Vernon after her husband completed his second term of office in 1797.

Following George's death in 1799, Martha continued to reside at Mount Vernon. In 1800 Congress granted her a lifetime franking privilege, which it continued to grant to any president's widow who applied for it. After Martha died in 1802, there was considerable discussion in Congress about burying the Washingtons in the capital city that bore their name, but instead she was buried beside George in a family tomb at Mount Vernon.

As wife of the first president of the United States, Martha Washington had no examples to follow. Although she was reluctant to assume a public role, her willingness to do so contributed to the eventual strength and influence of the position of first lady.

Congress sympathized with the movement and attempted to paralyze Washington by reorganizing the board of war, a body vested with the general superintendence of operations, of which Gates became the president; his chief of staff, James Wilkinson, the secretary; and Mifflin and Timothy Pickering, members. Washington was well aware of the hostility in congress, of the slanders spread by Rush and James Lovell of Massachusetts, and of the effect of forgeries published in the American press by adroit British agents. He realized the intense jealousy of many New Englanders, which made even John Adams write his wife that he was thankful Burgoyne had not been captured by Washington, who would then "have been deified. It is bad enough as it is." But Washington decisively crushed the cabal: after the loose tongue of Wilkinson disclosed Conway's treachery, Washington sent the general on November 9, 1777, proof of his knowledge of the whole affair.

With the conclusion of the French alliance in the spring of 1778, the aspect of the war was radically altered. The British army in Philadelphia, fearing that a French fleet would blockade the Delaware while the militia of New Jersey and Pennsylvania invested the city, hastily retreated upon New York City. Washington hoped to cut off part of the enemy and by a hurried march with six brigades interposed himself at the end of June between Sir Henry Clinton (who had succeeded Howe) and the New Jersey coast. The result was the Battle of Monmouth on June 28, where a shrewd strategic plan and vigorous assault were brought to naught by the treachery of Charles Lee. When Lee ruined the attack by a sudden order to retreat, Washington hurried forward, fiercely denounced him, and restored the line, but the golden opportunity had been lost. The British made good their march to Sandy Hook, and Washington took up his quarters at New Brunswick. Lee was arrested, court-martialed, and convicted on all three of the charges made against him; but instead of being shot, as he deserved, he was sentenced to a suspension from command for one year. The arrival of the French fleet under Adm. Charles-Hector Estaing on July 1778 completed the isolation of the British, and Clinton was thenceforth held to New York City and the surrounding area. Washington made his headquarters in the highlands of the Hudson and distributed his troops in cantonments around the city and in New Jersey.

THE PAINTING SIEGE OF YORKTOWN *DEPICTS* GEORGE WASHINGTON *GIVING ORDERS TO HIS ARMY. THE SIEGE OF* YORKTOWN *ENDED THE FIGHTING IN THE AMERICAN REVOLUTION.*

The final decisive stroke of the war, the capture of Cornwallis at Yorktown, is to be credited chiefly to Washington's vision. With the domestic situation intensely gloomy early in 1781, he was hampered by the feebleness of Congress, the popular discouragement, and the lack of prompt and strong support by the French fleet. A French army under the comte de Rochambeau had arrived to reinforce him in 1780, and Washington had pressed Admiral de Grasse to assist in an attack upon either Cornwallis in the south or Clinton in New York. In August the French admiral sent definite word that he preferred the Chesapeake, with its large area and deep water, as the scene of his operations; and within a week, on August 19, 1781, Washington marched south with his army, leaving Gen. William Heath with 4,000 men to hold West Point. He hurried his troops through New Jersey, embarked them on transports in Delaware Bay, and landed them at Williamsburg, Virginia, where he had arrived on September 14. Cornwallis had retreated to Yorktown and entrenched his army of 7,000 British regulars. Their works were completely invested before the end of the month; the siege was pressed with vigour by the allied armies under Washington, consisting of 5,500 Continentals, 3,500 Virginia militia, and 5,000 French regulars; and on October 19 Cornwallis surrendered. By this campaign, probably the finest single display of Washington's generalship, the war was brought to a virtual close.

Washington remained during the winter of 1781–82 with the Continental Congress in Philadelphia, exhorting it to maintain its exertions for liberty and to settle the army's claims for pay. He continued these exhortations after he joined his command at Newburgh on the Hudson in April 1782. He was astounded and angered when some loose camp suggestions found expression in a letter from Col. Lewis Nicola offering a plan by which he should use the army to make himself king. He blasted the proposal with fierce condemnation. When the discontent of his unpaid men came to a head in the circulation of the "Newburgh Address" (an anonymously written grievance) early in 1783, he issued a general order censuring the paper and at a meeting of officers on March 15 read a speech admonishing the army to obey Congress and promising his best efforts for a redress of grievances. He was present at the entrance of the American army into New York on the day of the British evacuation, November 25, 1783, and on December 4 took leave of his closest officers in an affecting scene at Fraunces

Tavern. Traveling south, on December 23, in a solemn ceremonial immortalized by the pen of William Makepeace Thackeray, he resigned his commission to the Continental Congress in the state senate chamber of Maryland in Annapolis and received the thanks of the nation. His accounts of personal expenditures during his service, kept with minute exactness in his own handwriting and totalling £24,700, without charge for salary, had been given to the controller of the treasury to be discharged. Washington left Annapolis at sunrise of December 24 and before nightfall was at home in Mount Vernon.

In the next four years Washington found sufficient occupation in his estates, wishing to close his days as a gentleman farmer and to give to agriculture as much energy and thought as he had to the army. He enlarged the Mount Vernon house; he laid out the grounds anew, with sunken walls, or ha-has; and he embarked on experiments with mahogany, palmetto, pepper, and other foreign trees, and English grasses and grains. His farm manager during the Revolution, a distant relative named Lund Washington, retired in 1785 and was succeeded by a nephew, Maj. George Augustine Washington, who resided at Mount Vernon until his death in 1792. Washington's losses during the war had been heavy, caused by neglect of his lands, stoppage of exportation, and depreciation of paper money, which cost him hardly less than $30,000. He then attempted successfully to repair his fortunes, his annual receipts from all his estates being from $10,000 to $15,000 a year. In 1784 he made a tour of nearly 700 miles (1,125 km) to view the wildlands he owned to the westward, Congress having made him a generous grant. As a national figure, he was constrained to offer hospitality to old army friends, visitors from other states and nations, diplomats, and Indian delegations, and he and his household seldom sat down to dinner alone.

CONCLUSION

The motto *E Pluribus Unum*—"out of many, one"—was proposed by a Swiss-American patriot and immigrant named Pierre Eugene du Simitiere for the new American republic. Perhaps no three words could more encapsulate the complex and simple idea of the United States—that this was a country made up of many individuals, committed to living their own way and without a central despotism, yet their collective power is undeniable when they agree to make the right kind of compromises and work together.

The American Revolution may have been an inevitable outcome of social forces, personal convictions, and international disputes. It might also have been a historical accident, fanned by the political radicalism of a few Philadelphia intellectuals and ensured by the miscalculating British Empire. In either case, the Revolution set an example that would be explicitly followed in France and Haiti just several years afterward. In countless other countries around the world, words, phrases, and ideas from the American Constitution and Declaration of Independence have made their way onto placards and into slogans of revolutionary movements for more than two centuries. This shows that the American Revolution didn't just change the course of American history, but it brought the promise of a new kind of freedom into the world.

139

ACRIMONIOUS Caustic, biting, or rancorous especially in feeling, language, or manner.

APOCRYPHAL Of doubtful authenticity.

CAPITULATION A set of terms or articles constituting an agreement (as a treaty or convention) between governments.

CEDE To give up, give over, grant, or concede typically by treaty or negotiated pact.

CHANCELLOR OF THE EXCHEQUER A member of the British cabinet in charge of the public income and expenditure.

DEISM A rationalistic movement of the 17th and 18th centuries whose adherents generally subscribed to a natural religion based on human reason and morality, on the belief in one god who after creating the world and the laws governing it refrained from interfering with the operation of those laws, and on the rejection of every kind of supernatural intervention in human affairs.

EGALITARIAN One who believes in human equality.

EX POST FACTO Done, made, or formulated after the fact and on the basis of current premises, conditions, or knowledge.

FRANKING Marking (a piece of mail) with an official signature or sign indicating the right of the sender to free mailing.

FRIGATE A light boat propelled originally by oars but later by sails.

GARRISON To furnish with soldiers; to supply (a military post) with troops for defense.

IMPOST Something imposed or levied.

INSUBORDINATION The quality or state of being unwilling to submit to authority.

LEVIED Imposed or collected (as a tax or tribute) by legal process or by authority.

MANUMISSION A formal emancipation from slavery.

MENSURATION The application of geometry to the computation of lengths, areas, or volumes from given dimensions or angles.

ORTHODOXY Conformity to an official formulation of truth especially in religious belief or practice.

PRIMOGENITURE The eldest son's exclusive right of inheritance.

PROVISO An article or clause (as in a statute, contract, or grant) that introduces a condition, qualification, or limitation and usually begins with the word "provided."

PUNITIVE Inflicting, awarding, or involving punishment or penalties.

REMONSTRANCE An earnest presentation of reasons in opposition to something; specifically a document formally stating points of opposition or grievance.

RIPOSTE A retaliatory maneuver or measure; a counterattack.

SPECTRE Something that haunts or persistently perturbs the mind.

SQUADRON A unit of military organization.

SURREPTITIOUSLY In a furtive manner.

TARIFF A schedule of duties imposed by a government on imported or in some countries exported goods.

THREEPENCE The sum of three pennies.

BIBLIOGRAPHY

THE AMERICAN REVOLUTION

Richard L. Blanco (ed.), *The American Revolution, 1775-1783: An Encyclopedia*, 2 vol. (1993), is a valuable reference source. Edward Countryman, *The American Revolution* (1985), considers American social history in the explanation of how American resistance developed. P.G.D. Thomas, *British Politics and the Stamp Act Crisis* (1975), is a scholarly account of British objectives and methods, and *The Townshend Duties Crisis* (1987) is the most comprehensive account of this episode. Jerrilyn Greene Marston, *King and Congress* (1987), studies how Congress acquired formal "legitimacy" in the course of rebellion. Morton White, *The Philosophy of the American Revolution* (1978), analyzes the concepts that took shape in the Declaration of Independence. Jack N. Rakove, *The Beginnings of National Politics* (1979), interprets the complex politics of the Continental Congress.

Bernard Bailyn, *The Ideological Origins of the American Revolution*, enlarged ed. (1992), examines the transmission of English republican ideology and its American reception. John Richard Alden, *The American Revolution, 1775-1783* (1954, reissued 1987), is distinguished for its political and military analyses. Jack P. Greene (ed.), *The American Revolution: Its Character and Limits* (1987), contains a valuable collection of essays. Robert Middlekauff, *The Glorious Cause: The American Revolution, 1763-1789* (1982, reprinted 1985), examines the revolution from a somewhat older point of view than is now fashionable. Piers Mackesy, *The War for America, 1775-1783* (1964, reissued 1993), explains the British side of the war. J.G.A. Pocock (ed.), *Three British Revolutions: 1641, 1688, 1776* (1980), sets the American Revolution in the historical context of British experience. Military histories include John Shy, *Toward Lexington: The Role of the British Army in the Coming of the American Revolution* (1965), on the British army in America; Don Higginbotham, *The War of American Independence: Military Attitudes, Policies, and Practice, 1763–1789* (1971, reprinted 1983), which shows the interrelationship of military and political developments; Charles Royster, *A Revolutionary People at War: The Continental Army and American Character, 1775–1783* (1979, reissued 1986); and William M. Fowler, Jr., *Rebels Under Sail* (1976), on the American navy.

GEORGE WASHINGTON

George Washington's presidency is examined in Thomas G. Frothingham, *Washington, Commander in Chief* (1930); Forrest McDonald, *The Presidency of George Washington* (1974, reissued 1988), a study of the political and economic aspects of his administration; Frank T. Reuter, *Trials and Triumphs: George Washington's Foreign Policy* (1983), a useful introductory study; and Richard Norton Smith, Patriarch: *George Washington and the New American Nation* (1993), a detailed treatment of Washington's presidential days. Washington's role in determining the focus and development of the U.S. Constitution is discussed in John Corbin, *The Unknown Washington* (1930, reprinted 1972); and Glenn A. Phelps, *George Washington and American Constitutionalism* (1993).

Analyses of his military career can be found in Charles H. Ambler, *George Washington and the West* (1936, reprinted 1971); Hugh Cleland, *George Washington in the Ohio Valley* (1955); George Athan Billias (ed.), *George Washington's Generals* (1964, reprinted 1994), with an essay on Washington's generalship; Burke Davis, *George Washington and the American Revolution* (1975), an account of his role as military commander; Edmund S. Morgan,

The Genius of George Washington (1980), a brief study; Don Higginbotham, *George Washington and the American Military Tradition* (1985), an examination of his public life and life in the military prior to his becoming president; and Thomas A. Lewis, *For King and Country: The Maturing of George Washington, 1748–1760* (1993), with emphasis on the French and Indian War.

A brief biography of Martha Washington is Patricia Brady, "Martha (Dandridge Custis) Washington," in Lewis L. Gould (ed.), *American First Ladies* (1996), pp. 2–15. Books about George Washington that also treat Martha include Stephen Decatur, Jr., *Private Affairs of George Washington* (1933, reprinted 1969); Douglas Southall Freeman, *George Washington*, 7 vol. (1948–57; also published in an abridged one-volume version with the same title, ed. by Richard Harwek,1968; reissued as *Washington*, 1985); and James Thomas Flexner, *George Washington*, 4 vol. (1965–72), especially vols. 3 and 4.

INDEX

67, 76, 80, 101–102,
108, 113–114, 117,
118, 121, 122, 123,
132, 137

delegates from, 18, 59, 123

Virginia House of Burgesses,
119–120, 121

W

War of 1812, 86, 87, 109

Warren, Mercy Otis, 89, 96–98

Washington, D.C., 86, 92, 108,
110, 111

Washington, George, 33, 34, 36, 38,
42, 45, 49, 63, 73, 79, 80,
88–89, 103, 104, 105, 106,
107, 109, 113, 125–144

childhood and youth of,
114–119

as commander of
Continental Army,

19, 21, 25, 26, 27, 30,
31, 33, 113–114, 122,
123–124, 124–127

entry into politics, 120–122

freeing of slaves, 63–64

religious beliefs of, 74, 76,
77, 112

during Trenton-Princeton
campaign, 128, 130–131,
134–138

Washington, Martha Custis, 63,
92, 75, 132–134

West Indies, 4, 41, 42, 46

White House, 92, 108,
109, 111

Wilson, James, 8–9, 17

Y

Yorktown, 28, 38, 43,
136, 137